Explorations into Urban Structure

Publications in the City Planning Series

Institute for Urban Studies
University of Pennsylvania
Robert B. Mitchell, Director

HOUSING MARKETS AND PUBLIC POLICY
William G. Grigsby

EXPLORATIONS INTO URBAN STRUCTURE
M. M. Webber, J. W. Dyckman, D. L. Foley, A. Z.
Guttenberg, W. L. C. Wheaton, C. B. Wurster

STRUCTURING THE JOURNEY TO WORK
Howard S. Lapin

URBAN RENEWAL IN EUROPEAN COUNTRIES:
Its Emergence and Potentials
Leo Grebler

Explorations into Urban Structure

Melvin M. Webber
John W. Dyckman
Donald L. Foley
Albert Z. Guttenberg
William L. C. Wheaton
Catherine Bauer Wurster

Philadelphia

UNIVERSITY OF PENNSYLVANIA PRESS

7415

Printed in the United States of America

Foreword

This group of essays has grown out of a long-standing interest among the panel of authors. A few of us at Berkeley were originally encouraged to undertake a more systematic examination of the underlying conceptions about the metropolitan community by Harvey S. Perloff, Director of Regional Studies at Resources for the Future, Inc. During the period in which these essays were being written, the group was enlarged by John W. Dyckman's visit to Berkeley. We were all pleased to discover a community of interest in the puzzles we were struggling with, and we were all the more pleased to find that each of us had quite independently come upon a similar way of thinking about the metropolis and especially about the relations between its spatial and its nonspatial aspects.

We rather suspected then, and it may actually have been true, that it was the character of urbanization in the West that had set us to thinking in a common direction. Especially here in California one is perforce oriented to growth and to change; the weights of tradition and of sunk investments are relatively light; spatial and institutional forms are more dispersed; and physical distance stands as a relatively weak barrier to interaction. Indeed, it was the ease of communicating with our associates on the East Coast and elsewhere that made it so apparent to us that we were all members of the same intimate community, despite our spatial separation. Whether it was through interchange of ideas or through parallel evolution or through exposure to common stimuli, we and they had come to share a conceptual framework that defined a true community of interests. Subsequently, two of our East Coast intellectual neighbors, Albert Z. Guttenberg and William L. C. Wheaton, contributed essays to this symposium. Several others might have, for our community is growing rapidly, as the characteristics that may once have been California idiosyncrasies become common traits of urbanization elsewhere.

The current essays thus reflect a common conceptual thread that has been reinforced by a considerable amount of encouraging discussion. Nevertheless, it has been our deliberate intent to retain the individuality of these papers. No effort has been made to construct a unitarily interlocked argument, such as would be expected with single authorship. Instead, and in harmony with the very philosophical conceptions that bring the group together, the essays are somewhat independent and disparate; on some important issues, they reflect disagreement among the authors.

They are presented in the spirit in which they were written, as exploratory forays into well-trodden areas where, too often, familiarity has been mistaken for comprehension. In the following pages we have tried to present some different, and we believe crucial, ways of looking at the organization of urban communities—views that seek to get closer to the spatial, processual aspects of the community's social and economic life than do traditional city-planning approaches or the classical approaches of land economics, human ecology, and geography.

The reader will find few clean, operational procedures by which suggested measurements might be made; correspondingly, he will find but little empirical evidence presented to support these explorations. What we have to say is largely deductive and intuitive; our thinking is presented as hypotheses, rather than findings. If others see potential utility in the ideas expressed, we hope that they will want to contribute to pushing these explorations to the point where they can be empirically tested and, then, if they still appear useful, to the point where they can be applied in metropolitan planning.

Five of the essayists—Dyckman, Foley, Webber, Wheaton, and Wurster—are presently members of the City and Regional Planning Faculty at the University of California, Berkeley, where Dyckman is also Chairman of the Center for Planning and Development Research and Wheaton is Director of the Institute of Urban and Regional Development. At the time these essays were prepared, Dyckman and Wheaton were members of the City Planning Faculty at the University of Pennsylvania, where between 1954 and 1962, Wheaton also served as Director of the Institute for Urban Studies. Guttenberg is currently a city planning consultant in Washington, D.C.

We are indebted to those who criticized certain of the essays in early drafts: James S. Ackerman, Roland Artle, Henry Fagin, John D. Herbert, T. J. Kent, Jr., Richard L. Meier, Robert B. Mitchell, Jesse Reichek, Leonore R. Siegelman, and Jerrold Voss. We are especially indebted to Harvey Leibenstein and George Duggar, who conferred with the original Berkeley group during the early formulative period and greatly influenced our thinking, and to Harvey S. Perloff, who has been among our most provocative critics.

Grace Milgram, of the University of Pennsylvania's Institute for Urban Studies, has earned the gratitude and admiration of each of us for the care with which she edited the manuscripts and guided the volume through to publication.

The essay by Wheaton is based on a paper that was commissioned by Dr. Robert C. Weaver and Dr. Morton J. Schussheim, Administrator and Assistant Administrator of the U.S. Housing and Home Finance Agency. In an earlier version the paper provided a framework for discussion at the Administrator's Conference on Urban Expansion. We are grateful to Drs. Weaver and Schussheim and to the HHFA for their permission to publish this essay here. The essay by Guttenberg is based on a paper prepared for a seminar on urban structure sponsored by the Joint Center for Urban Studies of the Massachusetts Institute of Technology and Harvard University, June, 1961.

The essays by Foley, Webber, and Wurster were prepared with the assistance of a grant from Resources for the Future, Inc., to the Regents of the University of California. The grant, which was made within the framework of RFF's Regional Studies Program, is acknowledged with gratitude—the more because, for RFF, this represented a major departure from the traditional natural resource fields. They were in effect grubstaking a group of prospectors to dig in territory that was largely unexplored, where the assay was unpredictable, but which RFF and many others might find worth mining. We surely didn't strike gold, but we are confident that we have uncovered a few rich seams that now warrant further exploration.

M.M.W.

Berkeley, California
August, 1962

Introduction

As the instigator of the project that produced the studies that initiated this volume, I may be permitted some unsystematic comments on the current boom in systematic urban research and theory building. These essays are a small contribution to that wave, but their imaginative concern with various aspects of metropolitan structure is, I think, of fundamental importance. This focus can lead not only toward a more effective framework for intensive expert analysis. It can also begin to forge the missing link in public communication: a common image of the nature of the modern urban community, its essential purposes and how they can best be fulfilled.

Less than a decade ago it was the rare (and usually low-status) social scientist who regarded the problems of urban and regional development as worthy of his attention. "Useful" work was limited to the few studies that operating agencies and a handful of research-minded city planners were able to conduct. Now all this has changed. Throughout the country there is growing rapport between academic social scientists, who are increasingly interested in the development process and metropolitan policy issues, and professional planners who are increasingly concerned with the application of advanced theory and scientific techniques to their problems. In some cases there has been virtual amalgamation, with the traditional academic or professional labels becoming almost meaningless. Moreover, political and civic leaders are beginning to rely on the results of the new collaboration.

This is real and rapid progress, which brings new hope for the future of planning. But science is becoming so fashionable in planning circles that it may be worth pondering some of its limitations as a bright new tool for improving the urban environment.

In the first place, the demand for systematic knowledge derives largely, it must be remembered, from a sense of failure and frustration at the policy level. Where the public, the major decision-makers, and their experts tend to agree on what needs to be done to improve cities, and are fairly well satisfied with the results of these actions, there is little felt need for scientific research. This was much truer of postwar urban policies in northern Europe than in the United States, and it is one reason why they have been *doing* things which many Americans admire, while we are forced to devise complicated methods of finding out *what* we ought to be doing and how we might do it. However, the British, Dutch, and Scandinavians seem less able to cope with prosperity and the automobile than with their older problems, and they may soon be looking to us for guidance in setting up research institutes in urban and regional science of their own.

But failure is only in part due to lack of accumulated knowledge. It is also due to lack of effective new ideas, communication, and leadership. Planners have two quite different roles: as objective technicians and analysts, and as reformers—literally as both large-scale designers of the future environment and as political movers and shakers. In both roles advanced scientific methods can be very helpful, but they can also have serious weaknesses if not applied with equally great imagination.

Certain technical limitations are obvious. Social science has to deal with so many variables in the urban field that it can rarely provide a proven factual basis for any decision whatever. An ingenious researcher can usually find what he wants to find, and it is dangerous to generalize from a few studies, however brilliant or intensive. In the suburban field, for instance, Whyte and Gans reach quite different conclusions, in neither case directly related to policy determinations. The weakness of projective methods for future-oriented planning in a rapidly changing world is likewise all too evident. The depression-minded demographers and economists of the 1930's turned out to be entirely wrong; are our current prosperity-projecting experts likely to be much more accurate if the cold war happens to let up or turn into a hot war? And in computer operations particularly, the necessary reliance on quantifiable factors can readily lead to overweighting them or distorting their meanings, at the expense of equally important factors which do not lend themselves to statistical interpretation.

Of more basic importance to effective planning, however, is the inherent conflict between a skeptical scientific temperament and the temperament necessary for an effective reformer. By and large, science can only help to explain why things are the way they are. Since there are always good reasons, there is a tendency for good studies to make current conditions seem inevitable. And this can lead to a kind of paralysis with respect to issues which require bold innovation. As we have grown more sophisticated about our slums, for instance, it has become ever more difficult to think of anything better to do. In a field where there can never be full factual proof of what ought to be done in the future, moreover, too much respect for scientific methods means timidity in making positive inferences and bold judgments. Scientists hate above all to look foolish, but reformers have to take their chances. Finally, there is the danger of a highly romantic and unscientific faith in scientific evidence per se as a prime mover and persuader. It is all very well that the main function of planners is "to preside over the flow of information," but this means a lot more than just digging up facts. It means communicating facts, ideas, and judgments to the decision-makers in forms that will persuade them to change some of their most cherished institutions and practices.

That these captious and perhaps naïve warnings come from a congenital reformer without scientific training is obvious. But the limitations and dangers which I have suggested do not apply, by and large, to the papers in this book, despite the fact that they are quite theoretical, provide little information of immediate practical utility, and would hardly persuade the most academic senator to change his vote on urban legislation. These papers are more in the realm of exploratory ideas than pure science; but they tend to reflect a new synthesis, among able planners, between scientific methods and responsible leadership. Moreover, they are all significant efforts, from various viewpoints, to begin to fill a great gap in our common understanding which inhibits researchers, administrators, and reformers alike, as well as political leaders and the public: the lack of an accepted image of what a metropolis is and what it could or should be.

The traditional concept of "city" was something that any bright child could explain quite well. That image does not fit our present-day communities, but no one quite knows what we are getting, or could get, in its place. The rudiments of natural science, industrial production, and international politics have become part of the popular culture, but the ABC's of the metropolitan community have never been defined or communicated.

These studies are all concerned, in one way or another, with the pattern, structure, and dynamics of the metropolitan complex. They present bold hypotheses which lead toward viable concepts of the big alternatives for the future urban environment, big alternatives which can be refined and tested by scientific research on the one hand, and simplified for general understanding and public decision on the other. This is the kind and level of objective analysis which, translated into easier language and visualized in alternative physical plans, is most needed by urban critics and reformers, the would-be movers and shakers. Without such disciplined concepts, the fashionably influential ideas of desirable urban form and structure have shifted from one extreme of romantic rebellion to another within the past few decades: from the Garden City idolum, reacting against the horrors of the nineteenth-century Big City, to the opposite half-world of ACTION, "saving the central city" by glorifying its virtues and scorning or ignoring all the forces that favor some form of decentralization.

Now there are signs of a new and more sophisticated public concern with growth forces, the relationship between outlying development and central redevelopment, and the structure of metropolitan regions. But if we really know any more than we did before, it may be due less to all the statistics we have been turning out than to the fresh kind of thinking represented in this book.

CATHERINE BAUER WURSTER

Contents

Foreword

Catherine Bauer Wurster

INTRODUCTION   9

Donald L. Foley

AN APPROACH TO METROPOLITAN SPATIAL
  STRUCTURE   21

  I. The Nature of the Framework   23
    A Diagrammatic Introduction   23
    The Main Relationships   28
    Alternative Relationships That Might Be Stressed 33
    Extension of the Scheme: Form and Process 35
    Further Extension of the Scheme: Change over
      Time   39

  II. Contributions of the Framework   41
    Stress on Certain Relationships   41
    Framework for Hypothesis Formulation   44
    Reconciling or Subsuming Other Formulations 47
    Behavioral, Decision-Making Approaches   53

  III. Implications for Metropolitan Planning   56
    The Unitary Approach and the Adaptive Ap-
      proach   56
    Urban Planning: A Resumé of Trends and Influ-
      ences   63
    What Metropolitan Spatial Organization?   67
    The Potential Integration of the Two Approaches 71

Melvin M. Webber

THE URBAN PLACE AND THE NONPLACE
URBAN REALM   79

I. Conceptions of the Urban Place   79
   Conceptions of the City and Region as Places   81
   The City as a Communications System   84
   An Index of Cultural Wealth   87
   The Shortcomings of the Land-Use and Density
   Concepts   90

II. The Spatial Structure Trichotomy of Urban Places   95
    The Components of Spatial Structure   95
    A Descriptive Schema for Spatial Structure   102

III. Urban Realms—The Nonplace Communities   108
     The Interest-Communities   108
     The Urban Realms   114
     Directions for Empirical Observation   120

IV. The Relevance to Metropolitan Planning   132
    Concerning Territory, Place, Boundaries, and
    Governments   132
    The Classification of Centers   137

William L. C. Wheaton

PUBLIC AND PRIVATE AGENTS OF CHANGE
IN URBAN EXPANSION   154

I. The Investment Mix   155
   Volumes and Types of Investment   155
   Controlling Criteria of Decision   164
   Fact and Value in Market Decisions   167
   Decision Chains and Nonmarket Criteria   171

II. The Pluralism of Metropolitan Decisions   175
    Public Decision Processes and Institutions   175

Past and Present Decisions 179
Private Systems of Power 182
Decision-Making in the Mixed Economy 184

III. To Improve Rationality and Consensus 187
Guiding the Fact Component 187
Guiding the Standard Component 192
Some Conclusions 194

Albert Z. Guttenberg

THE TACTICAL PLAN 197

I. Functional Centrality as an Objective 200

II. Tactical Planning 202
The Goal Plan and the Tactical Plan 202
The Tactical Plan and Conventional Capital
Programming 203

III. Tactical Form—An Example 205
Regional Growth and Its Consequences 205
The Tactical Variant 208

IV. Perspectives 210
The Tactical Variant and the Private Interest 211
The Tactical Variant as an Urban Renewal Plan 213
The Tactical Planner and the Public 215

John W. Dyckman

SUMMARY: PLANNING AND METROPOLI-
TAN SYSTEMS 220

List of Figures

Figure   Page

An Approach to Metropolitan Spatial Structure

1   Selected aspects of metropolitan structure: a conceptual view   24
2a The main relationship, with functional organization (2A and 2B) as pivotal   30
2b An alternative relationship: primary concern for immediate physical environment (3A)   30
2c An alternative relationship: primary concern for values as to spatial arrangement (1B)   31
2d An alternative direct relationship between values (1A via 1B) and the physical environment (3B)   31
3   Form and process distinctions applied to metropolitan structure   36
4   Changes over time in metropolitan structure   40
5   Distinguishing characteristics of the unitary and adaptive approaches to metropolitan planning   59

The Urban Place and the Nonplace Urban Realm

1   Major causal links among urban spatial structure components   94
2   Regions and geographic divisions of the United States   115
3   Hexagonal schema of Christaller's system of central places   117
4   The structure of realms   119
5   The hierarchical continuum of realms   123
6   The interest-community composition of realms   124
7   An interest-community, by realm   125
8   An interest-community, by arbitrary realm divisions   125

19

List of Figures

9 An interest-community, by arbitrary realm divisions 126
10 Irregular profile through the United States, showing disparity of locational distributions of realm-
participants in one interest-community 128
11 The profile shown in Figure 10, weighted by content of information received by realm-participants
in one interest-community 129
12 Two hypothetical patterns of activity distribution 141

The Tactical Plan
Figure 1 201
Figure 2 206
Figure 3 209

List of Tables

Table Page

Public and Private Agents of Change in Urban Expansion

I Total Annual Public and Private Capital Outlay
Expenditure, by Function, in the Five-County
Philadelphia Metropolitan Area, 1957-1960 156
II Percentage Distribution of Annual Public and Private Capital Outlay Expenditure, by Function,
within Each of the Five Philadelphia Metro-
politan Area Counties, 1957-1960 158
III Percentage Distribution of Annual Public and Pri-
vate Capital Outlay Expenditure, by Function,
by County, for the Five-County Philadelphia
Metropolitan Area, 1957-1960 159
IV Number of Governmental Units by Type, Pennsylvania Part of Philadelphia Metropolitan Area,
1960 162
V Population Served by General Governmental Units
in Philadelphia Metropolitan Area, 1960 162
VI Summary of the 1959-1964 Capital Program by
Source of Funds, City of Philadelphia 163

An Approach to Metropolitan Spatial Structure

Donald L. Foley

For those studying metropolitan communities or planning for the future of these communities, the ability to communicate about the object of their concern is clearly of fundamental importance. There is evident need for a common conceptual framework and a common language for exchanging ideas and proposals.

This essay suggests the rudiments of a possible framework. Much of what we have utilized in this effort has been suggested before. But we think that this approach highlights certain questions and suggests modes of attacking these questions which may enhance our capacity to deal with and understand the spatial structure of metropolitan communities. We do not imply that the approach will satisfactorily deal with questions of a different order; some problems in this respect will be discussed in a subsequent section. The proposed framework may help to prevent certain misunderstandings or incomplete perspectives which otherwise might continue to plague us. Perhaps others will be stimulated to suggest further alternative approaches or modifications.

Our initial commitment was to explore what is meant by the "spatial structure" of metropolitan areas. Also, because of a direct interest in metropolitan planning, we started with a commitment to stress the physical environment of the metropolitan area. But it early became clear that the spatial arrangement of the metropolitan community as expressed through its physical form is by no means a closed system. This therefore led us to examine spatial structure within a broader setting.

"Metropolitan structure" thus became a more generic conceptual framework within which to view "metropolitan spatial structure." We broadened the framework to include aspatial views; a major sector deals with the functional organization of the community and another with cultural or value features of community life. This provides a framework sufficiently broad so that several categories of propositions serving to interrelate these sectors can be meaningfully encompassed.

The resulting framework reflects our effort to deal with a pair of questions: First, how is it possible to build a satisfactory conceptual bridge between the concern for *spatial* arrangement that underlies metropolitan planning and the essentially *aspatial* approaches to metropolitan and urban community organization taken by so much of social science and social philosophy? When metropolitan planners state that they seek to guide physical development, it is clear that it is the spatial organization of the metropolitan community that looms very large in their minds. Any general plan or master plan for a metropolitan area is in effect a policy statement as to how that area should be spatially arranged. But scholars of urban life who deal with urbanization and urban values tend to view the community in rather different and characteristically aspatial terms, conceived without direct regard for spatial arrangement.

Second, how is it possible to relate values and the physical environmental aspects of the metropolitan community? This is a pivotal question for metropolitan planning. Values tend to be general and amorphous and to defy ready translation into physical environmental terms. And yet the metropolitan planner legitimately asks how he may know whether the physical environmental scheme he is proposing facilitates or impedes the achievement of stated values. In all of this, values prove to be very elusive. They are difficult to pin down empirically. The planner needs a far more tangible set of requirements to be satisfied, which reflect the fundamental values that are agreed upon or taken for granted.

I. THE NATURE OF THE FRAMEWORK

A Diagrammatic Introduction

A conceptual framework that seeks to bridge these two kinds of gaps—between the aspatial and the spatial, and between values and the physical environment—is shown as Figure 1. While we intend the diagram to be reasonably self-explanatory, it may be helpful to identify the main points dealt with by the framework.

The distinction between "aspatial" (column *A*) and "spatial (column *B*) is a particularly important one for our purposes. Mainly, "spatial" refers to a direct concern for spatial pattern, i.e., for the pattern in which culture, activities, people, and physical objects are distributed in space. Conversely, "aspatial" refers to a lack of such concern for spatial pattern. This is not so much a deliberate choice to overlook spatial pattern as a positive focus on the characteristics and interrelationships of selected phenomena viewed within other frames of reference. For example, political scientists are far more concerned with governmental organization, with the personalities of key leaders, and with institutional relations between government and the rest of society than they are with the spatial patterns, as such, in which governmental or political activities occur. Similarly, economists focus on the economy

A Aspatial* Aspects	B Spatial* Aspects

	1A	*1B*
1 Normative or Cultural Aspects	Social values; culture patterns; norms; institutional setting; technology	Spatial distribution of culture patterns and norms; values and norms directly concerned with the qualities and determination of the spatial patterns of activities, population, and the physical environment
2 Functional Organizational Aspects	*2A* Division and allocation of functions; functional interdependence; activity systems and subsystems, including persons and establishments in their functional-role sense	*2B* Spatial distribution of functions and activities; linkages (functional relations spatially conceived); spatial pattern of establishments, by functional type
3 Physical Aspects	*3A* Physical objects: the geophysical environment, man-developed material improvements, people as physical bodies; qualities of these objects	*3B* Spatial distribution of physical objects; the resulting spatial pattern formed by this distribution of land forms, buildings, roads, people, etc.; distribution in space of varying qualities of physical objects

* We mean by "aspatial" no direct concern for spatial pattern (at whatever scale is being focused upon—in our case, metropolitan scale). Correspondingly, "spatial" means a direct concern for spatial pattern at the scale under consideration. (See also text discussion, pp. 23-24.)

Figure 1

Selected aspects of metropolitan structure: a conceptual view

as an entity and study its changing characteristics with little concern for regional or other spatial patterns within this institutional whole.

"Spatial" also tends to suggest a concern for spatial pattern at a designated scale. Thus we might differentiate an architectural scale with which an architect is most concerned, or an urban scale,[1] or, as in this essay, a metropolitan-wide scale. Hence, for our purposes at least, "aspatial" includes not only those conceptions that overlook spatial pattern of any sort but also those conceptions that focus on a spatial pattern at a different scale from that designated as primary. One may think, for example, of the spatial layout of a house and its yard, but at a scale so fine that it drops through our screen set up to sift out all but metropolitan-spatial considerations.

Introduced as a separate and cross-cutting classification is the distinction among the three levels or aspects, shown as *1, 2,* and *3* in the diagram. Within the first level, "normative or cultural aspects," we include the culture and the rules by which men live and the processes by which consensus is sought and achieved. This normative structure provides the social unity that comes from shared understandings. As anthropologists and sociologists stress, the cultural component includes many tacit and assumed understandings. The very conceptualization of what are treated as general values involves relatively high-level abstraction. The normative aspect of urban life, in sum, includes both the formulation of goals and the designation and enforcement of approved means for seeking these goals.

By "functional organizational aspects" of metropolitan structure (the second level) we mean the structure by which diverse functions are allocated and integrated within a community or among communities. Functional organization, in contrast to culture and norms, tends to focus on the complementarity of different functions and roles and to deal more directly with ongoing activities and interacting people. This sector of the diagram is thus conceived as including activities and, hence, activity systems and subsystems. Thus we include production and distribution systems, systems by which public services are provided, etc., and also include the component roles and establishments which comprise functional units within these systems.

The "physical" aspects of metropolitan structure (the third level) embraces the geophysical base for community life; the man-built modifications of this base, including buildings, streets, and major facilities; and people as physical objects occupying space, requiring transportation, etc. The physical environment may be thought of as embracing those permanent or semipermanent structures that house or channel activities and movement within the metropolis.

Supplementing what the diagram shows, we assume for our purposes that the typical approach to the normative aspect of community life is essentially aspatial (i.e., that it mainly deals with values and norms without being directly concerned with spatial arrangements). For example, students of the city may seek to isolate those main values that residents see in the city when migrating there. But the identification of these values is not likely to provide direct clues to the city's spatial pattern. A high value on consumer goods may encourage certain kinds of manufacture and retail trade, but will give little indication as to whether factories and stores will be concentrated or dispersed within the urban area. On the other hand, a stress on home ownership, by its implicit emphasis on low-density development, may suggest a rather dispersed urban pattern. In the context of our framework, we have placed the normative aspects of community structure essentially in cell 1A.

Cell 1B, by contrast, encompasses two variants: the spatial pattern by which cultural traits are distributed and those somewhat special values and norms that bear directly on the character of the spatial patterns of communities, with their populations, their activities, and their physical bases. Geographers, urban sociologists, and land economists, for example, share interests in the former. Included are the ecological studies of the spatial distribution of the living patterns of various subcultures, either ethnic groups or social classes. One can distinguish what the anthropologist has termed culture areas (or subareas). The study of values dealing with spatial patterns is the province of certain branches of aesthetics and a phase of what we may term the culture of cities.

We consider the physical environment to be space-consuming and space-defining, and hence as encompassed mainly by cell 3B of the diagram. The physical environment provides a permanent or semipermanent spatial pattern that is easily described in map or plan form. (That residents and visitors must carry some image of this spatial pattern in order to orient themselves and to move around readily is germane, but shades well into Cell 1B, insofar as normative as well as perceptive reactions are involved.) The very permanence of most of the physical environment promotes a stability of pattern and, indeed, a sense of tradition and of symbolism adhering to the pattern.

We treat cell 3A as of minor importance for purposes of our analysis. Within this conceptual category we posit those aspects of the physical environment that describe the physical objects in the metropolitan environment but which do not define or depict that environment's spatial pattern. For example, we can contrast the respective physical compositions of a Nevada city and a New England city, citing climate, trees and plant life, soil conditions, building materials and styles, housing quality, physical appearance of residents, etc. —but short of a direct concern for the respective spatial patterns of these two cities. Within this cell we include such characteristics as texture and color, and those qualities which provide symbolic clues to the meaning or use of structures and land coverage (e.g., clues to whether a building is used for governmental, religious, recreational or residential purposes, or whether land is used for agriculture or for processing).

A main feature of the resulting framework is the pivotal place of functional organization in mediating the relationship between the norms and values that we share and physical environmental planning (i.e., between top and bottom in the diagram), and in providing a particularly strategic point to analyze the transition between aspatial and spatial (i.e., from right to left, or left to right).

In particular, the conceptual framework allows us to examine the major conceptual gap between cell *1A* and cell *3B* of the diagram. Our challenge is to bridge this diagonal gap. The main S-shaped line of reasoning to which we move and upon which we place heavy emphasis for certain analytic purposes will be discussed below. (Figure 2a, page 30, will also show this.)

We shall now discuss possible analytic chains of reasoning which our framework (as summarized by the diagram in Figure 1) suggests.

The Main Relationships

While alternative emphases on relationships will be suggested below and are shown as Figures 2b, 2c, and 2d, the conceptual framework we have developed particularly serves to bring out the main, S-shaped set of relations depicted in Figure 2a. The spatial sector of the normative and the aspatial portion of the physical environmental are de-emphasized in this particular approach. Hence these cells are shown in dotted lines in Figure 2a.

In this particular approach the chain of relationships extends from *1A* to *2A* to *2B* and thence to *3B*. Or, in the reverse direction, from *3B* to *2B* back to *2A* and up to *1A*. It is clear that *2A* and *2B* are of critical importance in translating between values and the physical environment.

Starting from the values end, the first relationship, *1A* to *2A*, is particularly amenable to sociological investigation. It deals with the interplay of values and norms, on the one hand, and the functional organization of the metropolitan area, on the other. We could expect that the functional organization would facilitate rather than impede the values most sought, insofar as inevitable conflicts of values are themselves sufficiently resolved. According to sociological findings, the functional organization of our cities tends to change in various respects more rapidly than our values. This was dramatically phrased by Ogburn as "cultural lag." Major forces for change in functional organization include population growth and redistribution, technological innovations, violent swings in the business cycle, war, and income redistribution. In the sphere of business organization we have many examples of continuing and deliberate attempts to reorganize firms so as to meet redefinitions of functional demands. In other phases of our functional organization, such as the organization of religion and of the family, we have a closer reliance on traditional and often deep-seated patterns which may be more closely geared to a corresponding value structure. But in all institutional spheres there are very dynamic factors at work to bring about change. Generally, we see these changes first in the functional organization sector and only gradually, often with noticeable lag, do these become reflected in the values of society.

The second step, from functional organization aspatially viewed (2A) to functional organization spatially conceived (2B), would logically seem to fall well within the purview of the social sciences but actually has not been intensively dealt with in any systematic way. It is very possible that researchers in the city planning field could spark further work on this or contribute important approaches and findings themselves. The key question is how to examine the implications of alternative spatial arrangements on the functioning of given units of social organization. At the metropolitan community level, this is to ask in what alternative ways a metropolis may be spatially structured and with what relative facilitating or restricting of activities as indicated by the effect on the functional organization (2A) and, indirectly, the values (1A).

While the factors making for change in social organization aspatially also affect the spatial organization, certain forces, particularly those relating to the technology of transportation and communication, are at work modifying the spatial pattern (cell 2B) which, in turn, feeds back strongly on the organiza-

DONALD L. FOLEY

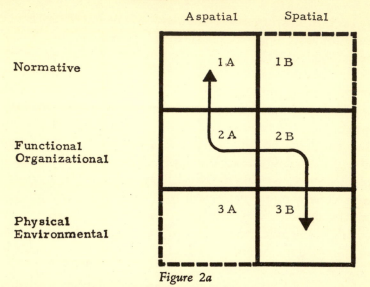

Figure 2a

The main relationship, with functional organization (2A and 2B) as pivotal

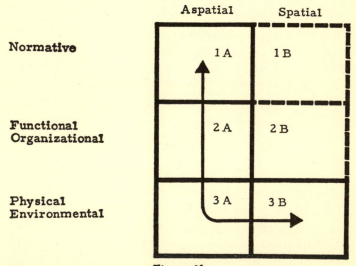

Figure 2b

An alternative relationship: primary concern for immediate physical environment (3A)

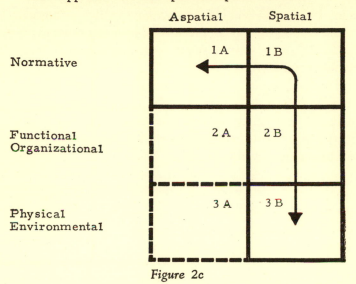

Figure 2c

An alternative relationship: primary concern for values as to spatial arrangement (1B)

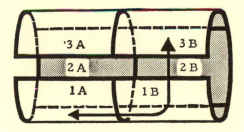

Diagram is rolled around so that the physical environment is placed next to the normative level. (The functional level is still in, but remains in the background.)

Figure 2d

An alternative direct relationship between values (1A via 1B) and the physical environment (3B)

tion within cell 2A. Hence, we have a lively interplay between certain functional, processual, or organizational changes in the 2A sector and the spatial arrangement of this organization in the 2B sector.

The final relation to be examined is that between functional organization spatially viewed (2B) and the physical environmental base spatially viewed (3B). In many ways this is a hand-in-glove sort of relation with the activities being snugly accommodated by the physical facilities. But the distinction between the activity system as it is spatially organized and the strictly physical spaces and channels—structures, outdoor spaces, streets, port facilities, etc.—is an important one. Physical facilities once developed tend to be either fixed or expensive to alter. The volumes, kinds, and distribution of activities, however, may shift considerably over the years. These shifting activities may adapt to their facilities; they may be seriously restricted by their facilities; or they may be forced to move from old facilities to newly developed ones. We are all familiar with the impact of extensive automobile use on street systems built in pre-automobile or early-automobile periods. We know less about the effectiveness with which other kinds of facilities built at an earlier period have managed to handle industrial or business operations, residential activities, or other urban-based activities. We know amazingly little of how the centers of older metropolitan areas function. Neither do we understand how the Los Angeles type of pattern really works.

City planning research has a major stake in the exploration of this step between 2B and 3B. For the physical environmental pattern, once fixed, would seem to constitute a forceful determinant, having impacts or providing restraints on the spatial patterning of activities and, via the kinds of relationships we are discussing, on the functional organization of the community.

Alternative Relationships That Might Be Stressed

In the reasoning we have just discussed, a conscious concern for over-all spatial organization is implied. The physical environment might then be shaped to accommodate this spatial organization.

A major variant is the possibility that those concerned with activities may concentrate on the particular immediate kind of setting they seek rather than focusing on the metropolitan spatial pattern. For example, home seekers or developers of residential tracts may be calculating with respect to structural type and lot size, but they may be little concerned with the larger spatial pattern of the metropolitan area. Nevertheless, a decision to promote single-family houses with 10,000 square-foot lots implies low-density development. This, in turn, has its own inevitable impact on the spatial arrangement of the metropolitan area. The relationships in this case are shown by Figure 2b, with the pivotal cells 2A and 3A.

Designers of the physical environment may be very much involved in this direction of interest. Architects, landscape architects, and site planners, for example, may be focusing on a quality of spatial development, but at a scale much below that involved in metropolitan planning. We quickly agree that planning would be incomplete without such concern for development at this smaller scale. But such planning at this smaller scale does suggest a distinctive chain of relationships.

Further variants are suggested by Figures 2c and 2d. These have, in common, reasoning which makes particular use of cell 1B of the diagram, that portion of the normative which deals with matters of spatial organization and pattern. This includes an important body of norms and the intellectual exploration of these norms that is central in the field of aesthetics. These norms serve to guide our reactions to, and help us to design, the spatial pattern of our communities. The norms may stress efficiency and provide a rationale for spatial arrangements that promote designated types of efficiency. They may refer to traditional and symbolic features of the physical environment and to questions of the preservation of, or change in, such features. They may embrace man's attempt to maintain a community environment at a human scale, and hence they may balk at or seek to reverse those rather relentless forces working to push all communities to ever huger sizes.

In Figure 2c, the stress is on relationships *1A* to *1B* and then via *2B* to *3B*. Figure 2d is similar, except that the chain of relationships goes directly from *1B* to *3B* without depending upon *2B* as an intermediate step.

The reasoning in Figure 2c serves as a complementary line of approach to the major chain of reasoning in Figure 2a. This is because at step *2B* in the major reasoning, there must inevitably be reliance upon values or other criteria in judging which spatial organization to favor. These can come in part from cell *1B*. Conversely, it is hard to conceive of values in *1B* that could be very strong, short of a thorough understanding of the meaning and content of cells *2A* and *2B*.

These modes of reasoning (Figures 2c or 2d) stress the importance of the physical environment as artifact. The physical environment in many important ways serves to perpetuate community traditions and to provide a sense of orientation within or to the community. Hence the physical base tends to carry or to symbolize important values. The physical environment in effect becomes aligned with culture in providing traditional continuity and in resisting recurring forces to change, such as are initiated particularly in the functional organizational sphere.

For reasons of brevity we have omitted some additional sets of relationships which might be stressed. For example, using those portions of our framework that are suggested in the wrap-around version of the diagram in Figure 2d, one could examine (or use as a mode of reasoning) the relationship between *1A*, the values and norms aspatially conceived, and *3A*, the physical environment aspatially conceived, and thence to *3B*, the spatial pattern of the physical environment. This resembles Figure 2b, but it omits a strong concern for functional organization. Additional sets of relationships may occur to the reader that we have not specifically discussed or diagrammed.

Extension of the Scheme: Form and Process

Up to this point we have identified several aspects of metropolitan structure while emphasizing spatial structure. We now introduce further distinctions. It is essential, for various purposes, to distinguish between (I) *form* (or morphological or "anatomical") and (II) *process* (or functional or "physiological") aspects of metropolitan structure.

Problems of definition loom immediately. If one conceives of "structure" as strictly morphological, the parallel treatment of processual aspects with form, as part of structure, becomes illogical and unorthodox. We do not want to have the term "structure" so restricted. We conceive of metropolitan structure as comprising both *formal* aspects—a static, snapshot view of the metropolitan community's pattern at any one point in time—and *processual* aspects—the ongoing functional relations of the metropolitan community. In such a view, the functioning of the community exhibits a pattern just as does the strictly morphological aspect of the community. With this conception, then, form and process may be readily treated as two complementary versions of structure.

Carrying through the framework already developed and adding this distinction between form and process provides us with a diagrammatic formulation as shown in Figure 3. This maintains the same primary distinctions between aspatial and

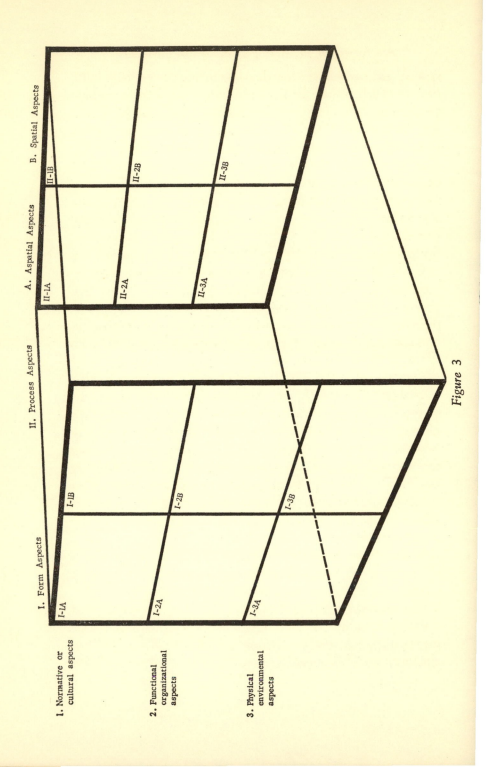

I. Form Aspects

II. Process Aspects

A. Aspatial Aspects

B. Spatial Aspects

I-1A I-1B

I-2A I-2B

I-3A I-3B

II-1A II-1B

II-2A II-2B

II-3A II-3B

1. Normative or cultural aspects

2. Functional organizational aspects

3. Physical environmental aspects

Figure 3

spatial, and carries forward the three levels previously identified. For each cell of the previous framework there are added counterpart aspects of form and process. On the aspatial side, for example, form connotes ideas of relationship and order (although without regard for space at a metropolitan scale); thus we speak of the form of government or the pattern of culture. On this aspatial side, process is very naturally dealt with, for process or function tend to be treated rather aspatially in most cases anyway. With respect to norms, for example, the processual aspect deals with the interaction involved in striving for consensus and with the social-psychological processes by which norms are developed, internalized by persons, and modified or rejected.

On the spatial side of the framework, the formal aspects refer to the distribution of culture patterns, in the sense that anthropologists have termed culture areas; the distribution in space of the establishments conducting urban activities; and the spatial patterning of the physical environment. The processual aspects correspondingly encompass notions of the patterns *in space* of the interaction among persons and establishments, and of the actual and potential volumes of these interactions. Insofar as process inevitably occurs in space, it is the spatial pattern of activity location (form) that serves to establish the corresponding spatial pattern of interaction (process). Conversely, a sensitivity to the interactions that must be maintained has an essential bearing on the location of the activities.

If one takes a typical workday or workweek, the spatial patterning of commuting, shopping, school attendance, business contacts, and governmental activities shows up as an interaction web that ties together all of the households and other establishments in a metropolitan community. These establishments may of course be depicted as mere spots on a map of the metropolitan community; the processes by which the community functions may be envisioned as lines or threads among the spots. Particularly with the areally great separation of functions within American cities one only gets a full sense of what goes on if he can grasp the nature of the rhythmic flows in space, often on a daily or other rhythmic basis. One may observe the dynamics of the build-up and dispersion during each day of great masses of people and of tremendous concentration and diminution of activity in certain nonresidential centers.

Insofar as this framework (as shown in Figure 3) provides something of a vocabulary and a mode of expressing relationships, we might pause to note one further consequence. While it is possible to move diagonally among sectors within the framework, we think that this suggests incomplete steps in reasoning. We think that moving at all times parallel to one of the three outer planes of the "cube" forces fuller comprehension. Let us take an example. One could move from *II-2A* (dealing with functional organization, aspatially conceived, in the processual plane) to *I-3B* (physical environment, spatially conceived, in the formal plane). But this might fail to depict the full nature of the conceptual gaps that are being jumped. The chain of reasoning can be kept more rational if each of the three directional moves involved is taken one at a time. Interestingly, there are several alternative sets of steps possible. Thus we have these plausible alternatives (among others):

II-2A to *II-2B* to *I-2B* to *I-3B* (converting *from* functional interdependencies *to* such interdependencies in space *to* the spatial arrangement of activities *to* a formal view of the physical environment to accommodate these activities).

II-2A to *II-2B* to *II-3B* to *I-3B* (same as above, except *from* a processual view of functional relations in space *to* a processual view of the physical environment *to* a formal view of the physical environment).

II-2A to I-2A to I-2B to I-3B (converting *from* functional interdependencies *to* the formal organization for carrying these out
to the spatial arrangement of this organization *to* the spatial
pattern of the physical environment to accommodate the organization).

To be forced to state each step serves to clarify the entire
chain of reasoning.

Further Extension of the Scheme: Change over Time

We have yet to stress one further distinction: that between
short-term rhythmic processes, dealt with in the previous section, and long-range processes of growth and change, to which
we now turn. Metropolitan structure not only exists at a
given point in time and is in process within a given short
period of time, but also it evolves over time. During designated longer periods of time, metropolitan structure may exhibit rather marked evolution.

Without repeating the previous diagram in its full complexity, Figure 4 depicts the idea that metropolitan structure
changes over time.

The introduction of a sense of historical depth is important.
The metropolitan structure at any given period is heavily
dependent upon its structure at earlier periods. This suggests
again the two kinds of lags—cultural and physical environmental—to which we alluded in our first discussion of the
relations between the normative, the functional organizational,
and the physical environmental levels. *Cultural lag* refers to
the distinct tendency for the cultural framework to change
less rapidly than the functional organization. We can point
to many examples where technologically induced changes,
while accepted in a civilization that lays great stress on change,
are by no means accompanied by direct corresponding normative changes that provide a full ethical and legal adjustment
to the new situation. *Physical environmental lag* applies to

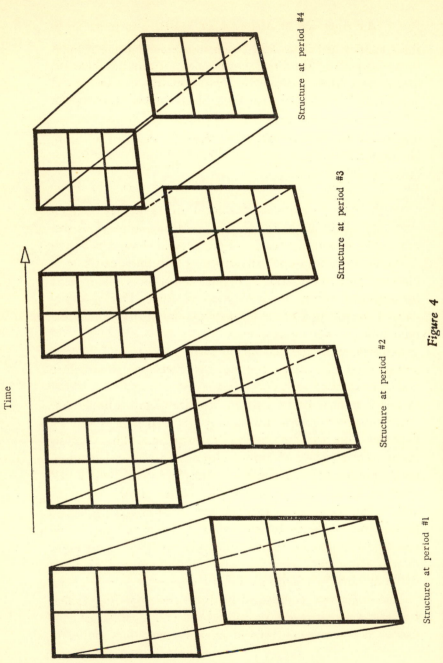

Time

Structure at period #1

Structure at period #2

Structure at period #3

Structure at period #4

Figure 4

the condition in which the physical environment, including the capital plant developed by man, fails to keep pace with growth and other changes in the systems by which activities are conducted. We are most dramatically aware of the inertia in our street system in the face of traffic increases, but we might also cite many other instances where physical facilities, because of their resistance to ready change, offer restraints on evolving activity systems.

II. THE CONTRIBUTIONS OF THE FRAMEWORK

We now wish to examine how this framework may serve planners and researchers. Three kinds of contributions will be suggested and each will be amplified in subsequent discussion. First, the framework stresses certain distinctions and relationships—particularly those dealing with functional and spatial organization—that urban and metropolitan planners and scholars might otherwise neglect or underemphasize. Second, with respect to various major relationships that we take to be of critical importance in understanding metropolitan structure, the framework encourages the formulation of hypotheses for further testing by research. And, third, the framework provides a setting within which otherwise scattered concepts and formulations may be seen in better perspective. Using the framework, we shall propose a tentative and rudimentary set of concepts and a pattern of relations among these concepts that might contribute toward future theoretical approaches to metropolitan structure.

Stress on Certain Relationships

The suggested conceptual scheme stresses activities and functional organization rather than relying too heavily or exclusively on values. This emphasis on activities is warranted because it furnishes the planner with a more palpable set of requirements for which to plan than do values, as they are usually presented. It is one thing to state that what is sought is a "balanced community"; it is quite another to translate this into criteria sufficiently tangible to provide planning guidelines. Similarly, a plea for more open space must be stated in terms of the desired qualities of this open space and the activities that it is to accommodate. It makes good sense to plan for the functional organization that is geared to facilitate high-priority values and then to design the physical environment so as to provide the best setting for this functional organization.

The proposed scheme also stresses the distinction and the corresponding close relation between the physical environment and the activity systems accommodated by this environment. It points out the crucial distinction and great conceptual gap between the realms of the spatial and the aspatial. And the framework re-emphasizes the complementarity of functional organizational aspects and the normative aspects of the metropolitan community's structure.

We submit that if a physical planner comes to think in terms of the proposed scheme he will be encouraged *to take into account the ways in which the physical environment* he recommends *facilitates or impedes various activity systems that are accommodated by that environment.* He should be encouraged to gain a thorough understanding of these activities as he engages in physical environmental design. The metropolitan planner might well make explicit the relationships with which he is most directly involved. He is thus encouraged to state the reasoning upon which he is relying. An explicit statement of his reasoning not only would clarify his own operations, both for his own purposes and for explaining his rationale to political leaders and the public, but also would communicate the chain of reasoning he is employing so that the logical steps may be susceptible to research check.

We are particularly impressed with the utility of clearly distinguishing between "physical" and "spatial." This prevents two possible misconceptions. First, it reminds planners and scholars that often when they say "physical" they may mean "spatial." The phrase "physical arrangement" sometimes refers to spatial arrangement. The physical planner in a real sense is a space planner; i.e., he plans how we might best arrange our environment and our activities in space. Second, it reminds us that components of urban structure other than the physical also have a spatial aspect. This may be true of functional organization and even normative structure. Often, when we speak of spatial pattern as if we were referring to the physical environmental setting, we may really be referring to the spatial patterns of the activities and of interpersonal relationships.

The scheme emphasizes that supporting research and planning are called for to supplement the physical planner's own efforts. The thorough study of the diverse systems and subsystems of activities within metropolitan areas requires the collaboration of varied social scientists and managerial and professional personnel. Too, complementary types of planning are clearly needed: program or activities planning, social planning, economic planning. By whatever terms and breakdown, planning responsible for the kinds, relative volumes, and organization of the activities to be conducted is called for to supplement and, logically, to precede physical planning. What is currently confusing is that the physical planners seek reasonably to bound their own scope, and yet know that, willy-nilly, they are assuming broad responsibilities for the kinds of activities and the patterns of social contacts facilitated by their physical designs.

Framework for Formulation of Hypotheses

The proposed framework, by its very nature, suggests major categories of relationships that form metropolitan structure. As indicated above, for example, four separate steps stand out in the S-shaped chain of reasoning. Each of these steps suggests a family of relationships. Thus, kinds of relationships are indicated about which corresponding hypotheses may be propounded.

From the physical planner's viewpoint, the first major group of hypotheses relate the physical environment spatially conceived (3B) and functional organization spatially conceived (2B). For example:

The spatial pattern of the physical environmental channels for communication and transportation will provide certain opportunities for and certain restraints on the spatial pattern of interaction within a functioning activity system.

An ongoing activity system has considerable capacity to bring about changes in the spatial patterns of its intercourse even within constant physical environmental spaces and formally provided channels. (This takes cognizance of the important role of informal communication within and supplementing a formal organization for communication.)

The same physical environment may, over time, come to accommodate rather strikingly different kinds, levels, and spatial patterns of communication and transportation.

As an activity system grows or otherwise modifies its functional organization, strains are inevitably introduced into the capacity of the physical environment to accommodate the system.

The spatial pattern provided by the physical environment inevitably influences the spatial pattern of interaction among persons or units of an activity system.

The interaction patterns of an activity system will reflect the channels as they are actually used rather than the channels as latently provided by the physical environment.[2] Correspondingly, distances may be altered.

Such hypotheses have in common a concern for the extent to which, or the conditions under which, the physical environment, through the spatial pattern it provides, either encourages or prevents the spatial arrangements of a functioning organization or system. To date, we have had relatively little systematic study of this, although obviously assumptions about this relationship intrude into what the physical planner undertakes. We suggest that a theory for metropolitan (and city) planning will need to give central consideration to this class of relationship.

The second group of hypotheses deals with the relation between functional organization spatially conceived (2B) and functional organization aspatially conceived (2A). We suspect that this category of hypothesis may in various ways be even more important than the 3B-2B group. Since the physical planner is so responsible for recommending spatial patterns, the critical question is how much difference it makes for the functioning of an activity system whether it is arranged in one spatial pattern or another. The metropolitan planner shares responsibility for exploring this question with a myriad of other researchers—those concerned with business administration, public administration, the economics of location, the design of transportation and communication systems, the effect on social relations, and so forth. The range of possible hypotheses in this class is great. Selected examples are suggested here:

The relative volume of potential spatial contact among any pair of persons or units within a system in space is directly proportional to the mass of the pair and inversely proportional to the distance between them. (Gravitational and potential theories fall in this general group of relationships.)

The chances of persons establishing social interaction are proportional to the amount of spatial contact between these persons.[3]

Units within the system will be more dependent upon other units in situations of large size and great density (as in the central area of a large metropolis) than will units that are spatially separated from the main nucleus of activities (as in an industrial satellite community many miles from the metropolitan center).

The more specialized the activity, the more accessibility to major centers in the metropolitan area it will generally require.

The more specialized the activity, the greater will be its market or service area (in terms of numbers of potential users).

In addition to formulating hypotheses which are restricted to a single step (3B to 2B, or 2B to 2A), we might suggest some that deal with the effect on 2A of manipulating 3B or the impact of changes in 2A on 3B. Such hypotheses logically entail at least two subhypotheses, examining one component of the total relation at a time. For example, we may ask: What will be the effect of a new freeway network on the functioning of a metropolitan area? This, in terms of our framework, readily divides into: (a) to what extent and in what ways will the new freeway system, as a physical facility (3B), encourage changes in the actual and potential spatial interaction patterns of the community (2B); and (b) what is the effect of these potential changes in spatial interaction patterns (2B) on the functional organization of the community (2A)? Analytically, it remains advantageous to deal with each relationship separately.

As for the third major relationship for which various hypotheses may be constructed—between functional organization aspatially conceived (2A) and normative aspects of community structure aspatially viewed (1A)—we move into spheres of inquiry more usually investigated by social and behavioral scientists and farther from the distinctive competence of the physical planner. This becomes difficult intellectual terrain, for there is unquestionably no one-to-one relationship between values and norms on the one hand and functional organization on the other.[4] The values of a society exert certain influences on its functional organization. Conversely, changes in the functional organization suggest potential impacts on societal values. Strains may be generated if the two components change at differing rates. Since we have been particularly concerned with the spatial structure of the metropolitan community, we shall not deal further with this relation, which is essentially aspatial. It continues to be the subject for investigation by sociologists and other social scientists.

Still other relationships are suggested by our conceptual framework. Some of these we indicated as alternatives in Figures 2b, 2c, and 2d above. Relationships involving norms and values in their spatial sense, or in the sense that they deal with space, are important. The symbolism of the physical environment and of space as defined by the physical environment deserves much further study. In what way does the physical environment carry or suggest values? What are the social-psychological effects of various environmental spatial patterns?

Reconciling or Subsuming Other Formulations

In developing this conceptual framework we have been influenced by the conceptual approaches of other researchers, and we have sought where possible to subsume these other formulations within a single framework. Let us now identify how some other recent contributions relate to our approach. The reader should bear in mind that there are some differences in scale between our primary concern for a metropolitan level of phenomena and the interest of some others with a smaller scale. But in an analogous sense the other approaches to be discussed bear directly on our own work. The examples dealt with in this section suggest existing or potential congruence with this present approach. In a following section we shall also discuss other important approaches which are less congruent; and this poses certain questions regarding the limitations of our approach.

We first want to express our intellectual indebtedness to Robert B. Mitchell, Chester Rapkin, and John Rannells for their work on land use and on movement systems.[5] The present framework has taken their approaches into account, expanding in some directions not taken by them but not restating what they have already focused upon. Their great contribution was to outline the possibilities of conceptualizing functional organization in its spatial aspect. The Mitchell-Rapkin terms—"establishment," "linkage," "movement systems," and "land use"—center on the 2B aspect of our framework. Then they adroitly deal with the relations between 2B and 3B, calling attention to the confusion as to what "land use" comprises. Rannells also picks this up, and in a chapter entitled "The Physical Setting" he discusses the relations between activities (2B) and their physical accommodations (3B). Mitchell and Rapkin also deal effectively with the relation between 2B and 2A, tracing back to the functional relations and the institutionalized organization (e.g., in marketing) and showing how the spatial arrangement of establishments relates to this functional organization. Rannells summarizes this when he asserts:

Although establishments are the most nearly fixed entities in the whole flux that we are seeking to comprehend, it is possible and even necessary to study them in the first instance without regard to their location. . . . All the routines of individuals . . . [and all] the relationships in which an establishment is concerned . . . can best be understood by setting up system patterns, diagrammatic statements of activities and patterns. . . . Such diagrams show systematic relationships which are valid without regard to location.[6]

This suggests the advantages of studying functional organization in its aspatial aspect prior to grappling with questions of spatial arrangement.

The Festinger, Schachter, Back study of two adjacent student housing projects at M.I.T. focused mainly on group structure in an essentially aspatial sense. But quite deliberately and certainly imaginatively, the authors elected to study the spatial ecology of group formation.[7] Festinger and his colleagues examined the influence of the spatial arrangement of the physical buildings, 3B, on the number of passive contacts (i.e., chance meetings) in the 2B category, and the further relation between the number of passive contacts, 2B, and more established social relationships, 2A. Thus, by utilizing the 3B to 2B to 2A reasoning channel that we have emphasized, these researchers established that the pattern of the physical environment influenced the number of chance contacts, and that this in turn was positively associated with friendship patterns.

In A. Benjamin Handler's stimulating essay, "What Is Planning Theory?," he proposed three frameworks as central to a theoretical approach to planning.[8] The first deals with the allocation of capital, relying on the criterion of economic efficiency; the second with goals, with human needs and values; and the third with forms. Handler's first framework, for dealing with the allocation of capital, reflects a viewpoint different from our own, but does nevertheless depend upon assumptions as to the relevance of economic efficiency (a possible value within 1A of our scheme) and the conceptual convenience of positing an activity system (2A). His second framework, goals and values, falls within our 1A. And what Handler seems to mean by form, as used in his third framework, is spatial arrangement. His suggested three-part breakdown of this third framework shows a close congruence with the spatial (B) side of our own schema. We quote from him to show this correspondence.

The framework of forms operates with three basic considerations, which may be viewed as subframeworks requiring to be fused. The first deals with problems of engineering and technology—the use and combination of materials, mechanical structures of all sorts, soil and topography, microclimate, use of plants and other natural features. [This matches our *3B* cell closely, and perhaps also includes part of *3A*.] . . . The second deals with problems of functioning. Basically this is question of use—who and what; under what circumstances and conditions; scope, character and timing of activities. It is a matter of so relating capital goods and their components to each other and their environment as to facilitate the movements and functions of people and things. [This is squarely within our *2B*, and expresses concern for the relations between *2B* and *3B*, and *2B* and *2A*.] The third deals with problems of looks—achieving a system of relationships in terms of appearance from various viewpoints and under varying conditions." [This falls within our *1B* cell.] [9]

Kevin Lynch, in two articles (the first written with Lloyd Rodwin) and, less directly, in his book *The Image of the City,* has spelled out approaches to urban or metropolitan form or pattern. In an unpublished paper he has also conveniently summarized a possible classification system.[10] He has sought to provide a vocabulary of concepts and terms and a way of using these. His main categories, deliberately arranged so as to correspond with our own framework, may be summarized as follows:

Our Categories	*Lynch's Terms*
Cultural or normative aspects	Objectives, goals criteria
Functional organizational aspects	Activity a. Localized activity b. Flow
Physical aspects	Physical facilities a. Adapted space b. Flow system

He also suggests various features of spatial pattern, such as grain, focal organization, and accessibility. He discusses alternative spatial patterns substantively, and points out ways by which the analysis of the patterns of specific metropolitan areas may be undertaken.

In terms of the main categories employed, his approach appears to be congruent with ours. In suggesting features of spatial pattern to examine and in carrying out his case studies of Boston, Newark and Los Angeles, described in *The Image of the City,* he has carried his scheme much further, and in particular has pushed ahead with problems of empirical measurement. But in one or two important respects, we think he could gain by taking into account the structured relationships suggested by our framework. First, he lapses overly simply into treating metropolitan spatial pattern as *a* phenomenon, and rather assumes that the activities so closely correspond to the physical facilities that to deal with one—and particularly the latter—is to deal with both. In their paper, he and Rodwin, for example, explain that they will focus on urban physical patterns because this is where most planners currently are involved. They go on to discuss various physical patterns related to goals or criteria. This is unclear and even misleading. Many times when they identify alternative patterns—of physical facilities, presumably—this makes sense only if one infers that it is in the conduct of activities that interaction takes place and that interests are pursued. Second, like many planners and urban researchers, Lynch fails to differentiate between "physical" and "spatial." Third, perhaps related to an underemphasis on activities, Lynch does not openly distinguish between and relate the spatial and the aspatial. We never get any full sense of the dynamic give and take between spatial patterns of activities and the institutional and functional organizational character of these activities in their spatial structural aspect.

Lynch faces a possible problem, too, in the relation between those goals or criteria which rather naturally focus on spatial pattern (for example, accessibility) and those that do not directly refer to spatial pattern (for example, democracy). A case can be made for pressing the distinction.

Our main suggestion is that Lynch consider a relatively greater emphasis on the *spatial pattern of activities* (2B), providing an important link between the pattern of the physical facilities (3B), the aspatial organization of activities (2A), and the two normative aspect cells (1A and 1B). Otherwise, he tends to end up discussing a physical environmental spatial pattern which in itself is mainly important because it accommodates activities (although he may well argue, in a different vein, that it has intrinsic importance as visual environment).

Albert Z. Guttenberg, in his "Urban Structure and Urban Growth," [11] provides a stimulating contribution, but seems unduly to handicap himself by somewhat unclear definitions of terms. For his purposes, "structural components" are physical facilities and transportation capacity; "form" is the pattern that these structural components make on the ground. The relation between physical facilities and activities is not recognized.[12]

The outstanding series of volumes in the New York Metropolitan Region Study have placed heavy emphasis on the functional organization-activity cells of our framework.[13] In general the strategy in the study has been to examine the past growth, the current momentum, and the likely future growth of various segments of economic activity within the New York Region (2A), and then to examine the prospects for spatial redistribution of these projected volumes of activities within the Region (moving over into 2B). The study did not place particular emphasis on the physical environment (or on physical planning), so that the full implications of likely changes in 2B for 3B were not investigated. Correspondingly, the full feedback of influences from a constraining or facilitating physical environment was not examined. In this series of volumes the members of the research team have assumed roles as observers and forecasters, and have not sought to identify what the governmental policies for guiding the region ought to be. (We shall comment further regarding normative vs. positivistic approaches in the final section.)

Our contention is that the framework suggested in this paper provides a broad setting within which these respective contributions could meaningfully be viewed. In some instances, a greater reliance on this framework might help to clarify or generalize these others. It is to some important approaches that cannot be so readily reconciled with the proposed framework that we shall now turn.

Behavioral, Decision-Making Approaches

The present conceptual framework was, as indicated above (pp. 21-23), intended to facilitate our approach to two questions. It should be clear that the same framework will by no means do all things for all purposes. Admitting this, certain questions may be raised: Can this framework be reconciled with other approaches that have been directed to different questions? Conversely, is it in any fundamental sense at odds with other approaches?

An important class of studies now being pursued in increasing number examines the decision-making behavior involved in the development of metropolitan areas. Several large-scale metropolitan transportation studies—the most notable current example being the Penn-Jersey Transportation Study—are being conducted in this spirit. Recent fine summaries and discussions of such studies are offered by Harris,[14] Wingo,[15] and Webber.[16] We turn to the question of how such behaviorally oriented approaches relate to the framework we are proposing.

A key characteristic of the behavioral approach, as applied to location theory and to land use and transportation models, is its insistence on disaggregation, on getting down to the level of the actions of householders, executives, workers, etc., as they make decisions in their own interests or on behalf of their organizational units. This contrasts to an aggregative approach in which the characteristics and changes of large numbers of persons or organizational units are measured and reported. Much demographic and ecological analysis is aggregative. Between the two extremes, our framework leans more toward the aggregative. Hence there may be certain possible difficulties in adapting it to a disaggregative, behavioral approach.

A behavioral approach to explaining changes in urban spatial structure over time also implies a concerted focus on the process of development.[17] In seeking to unravel the discrete threads of decision and action in the political economy, the behavioral approach recognizes the complexities of locational choice and market interplay in competing for favored position. Our brief discussion of changes over time (pp. 39-41, above) was more in the vein of viewing a time series of static portrayals, and was thus not directly geared to accommodating the decision-making orientation of the behavioral studies. Our framework is better adapted to the study of daily or near-daily process or flow within the metropolitan area (see pp. 37-38) than to viewing the dynamic process of long-term development.

The behavioral model, in focusing on decision-makers, throws the spotlight on the actor. This calls for an action schema. Simply put, our framework, in grappling with other questions, has not also provided a fully congenial setting for a strictly behavioral approach. We have no separate cells within our framework where the actor—and his motivations and outlook—clearly fits.[18] We have placed within our functional organization cells (*2A* and *2B*) both functional organization and activity systems. Within the concept of an activity system we have included functional roles, households, business establishments, and other organizations, but only as components of the system. We have focused on the systems. Our framework does suggest two important contributing aspects of behavior: a normative context (*1A* and *1B*), with the high probability that a significant portion of these norms are in fact internalized by actors or serve as a social control over behavior; and the structure of functional roles held by actors (in *2A* and *2B*).

Any distinction between aggregative and disaggregative can be misleading. At one extreme one can examine total population trends or project estimated increases in housing units. At the other, one can study consumption behavior and analyze its likely implications for the character of surburban development. The study of functional organization, given so central a place in our framework, might contribute an important middle ground between the extremes. In seeking to understand the future prospects and character of a metropolitan center, it is essential to view this center as facilitating the operation of a number of interlocking subsystems of activity. To put the main burden of analysis on a behavioral approach to location decisions may fail to get at the nature of organizational operations and linkages. At the other extreme, a strictly aggregative reliance on projecting gross statistics as to floor space, sales volume, etc., is deficient, since it fails to get at the likely behavior of the many decision-makers involved and the probable changes in functional relations among establishments and persons.

III. IMPLICATIONS FOR METROPOLITAN PLANNING

Faced as we are with serious renewal and developmental problems and confronted with prospects for continuing vigorous growth during the coming decades, we may look forward to an important and lively effort attempting to guide the development of each of our large metropolitan areas. Ever more planners, researchers, political leaders, and public administrators will be drawn into this activity. But metropolitan planning as an evolving institutional form is still in an extremely fluid state.

One traditional approach to metropolitan planning, borrowed from planning at lesser (i.e., urban and architectural) scales, is for a designer—or, more likely, a design team—to be given responsibility for preparing a plan for an appropriate governmental unit. Such an approach we may label *unitary*. Another approach, involving the decentralized decision-making of the urban real estate and land market and the policies and controls of various governmental units, may be designated *adaptive*. We shall discuss each of these, relating them to the framework already presented, and considering the prospects for their reconciliation. Finally, we shall propose an alternative approach, reflecting the framework of the previous two sections.

The Unitary Approach and the Adaptive Approach

The essence of the *unitary* approach, as this relates to urban and metropolitan planning, is to view the city or the metropolitan community as having a spatial, physical form that can be grasped and reduced to maplike graphic presentation. Planning is viewed as an activity dedicated to forming a picture of a future physical environmental pattern for a community and to fostering such development and control measures as will best ensure that the community will develop toward that future pattern. In short, a future spatial pattern is proposed as a goal.[19] The traditional means for communicating this future goal is the general plan, comprehensive plan, or master plan. Implicit in this unitary approach is the assumption that there will be a reasonably centralized governmental authority to prepare, approve, and carry out such a plan.

The *adaptive* approach to urban or metropolitan planning views the city or the metropolitan community as a complex interaction of diverse and functionally interdependent parts, with the parts evolving over time as they seek to adapt to the ever-changing contexts around them. This approach focuses on process, particularly the interactions that take place on a daily or short-term cycle—such as commuting, shopping, weekday business dealings, week-end recreational trips and activities, etc.—rather than on a longer-term cycle. Metropolitan planning, from this point of view, would seek first to gain a full understanding of how establishments and households interact (via the myriad actors involved), and how the metropolitan area develops over time. It then would seek to identify alternative development policies and to examine the probable implications of each in the light of certain established criteria as to desirable future conditions or optimal decision-making conditions. Planning, according to this approach, would seek to influence various of the development forces at work rather than aiming for a future metropolitan form as a goal.

In simplest terms, perhaps, this is a distinction between product and process. For the unitary view reflects in particular a product-design approach, flowing logically from the best traditions of architecture and the related design fields, that sees its mission as the design and the production of a future physical environment. In this spirit, quite naturally, planners prepare plans for this future physical form. That the plans may be diagrammatic and general, so that they must be supplemented by more detailed blueprints before construction can proceed, takes them no less out of the tradition. The planner is serving as executive architect and establishing certain general ideas and standards to which subsequent architecture and public works are expected to conform. Within such an envelope, precise plans may be given considerable leeway. Essentially, the unitary approach aims to create a future product, a physical environment for the city or the metropolis.

The adaptive view focuses on the processes by which persons and activities interact and, in particular, on the processes by which changes are introduced that will affect the future character of the city and the effectiveness with which persons and activities will be able to interact in this future situation. In the adaptive view, great emphasis is placed on the economy, broken into its diverse and interacting markets, as an allocative and decision-making mechanism. This view also recognizes that ours is in reality a political economy and that a sophisticated understanding of the role of government and of political decisions is also essential. Indeed, the rationale for adaptive planning recognizes that it is government's responsibility to guide the development process toward selected goals judged to be publicly desirable. In line with this adaptive planning approach, the creation of a better physical environment is not necessarily *the* major goal. The goals may embrace a range of desiderata relating to social life, to the economy, and to qualities of the total environment provided by the metropolitan community.

Figure 5 summarizes a number of salient characteristics of the two contrasting approaches.[20] These approaches are presented as ideal-type concepts being deliberately portrayed in purer form than ever found in real life. This has the ad-

Nature of the Characteristic	Unitary Approach	Adaptive Approach
1) The plan toward which planning works	Long-range locational-physical plan: the portrayal of a metropolitan spatial form for the future as desirable goal.	Policies and proposals constituting courses of action, to influence metropolitan development.
2) Substantive focus	Locational pattern of activities and the physical characteristics of the metropolis, taking into account social and economic goals; guiding controls to ensure that development will accord with desired character.	Social economy of the metropolis, including opportunities and standards for living, cultural and business activities, etc.; the public and private decision-making mechanisms by which development takes place.
3) Methodology	Intuitive-synthetic-political; aggregative; strong design influence; focus on product.	Empirical-analytic-economic; disaggregative; social science influence; focus on process.
4) Underlying assumption as to the basis for community solidarity	Solidarity results from consensus: a normative view of what is desirable.	Functional integration: solidarity results from the integration of diverse parts and viewpoints.
5) Assumptions regarding the political economy	Necessarily strong and fairly centralized role for government (the mix as between local and nonlocal subject to considerable variation); market decisions important but to be kept under control.	Decentralization; pluralistic political economy, with market-type decisions very important; governmental responsibility to provide leadership regarding prime-mover developments and to ensure working of economy in public interest.
6) Assumptions as to knowledge about the future	Precise knowledge irrelevant; strong design commitment and political leadership can provide self-fulfilling prophecy.	In view of complexity of the present and the essential unknowability of the long-range future, focus is on the near future and the directions of influence, subject to successive adaptation as the future unfolds.
7) Implicit aesthetics of spatial arrangement	Articulation: the designation of centers, the strong demarcation of circulation channels and internal boundaries, the clear bounding of the community so as to distinguish between city and country. Preferably treating designs as though they were reasonably final, with implication that disturbing overgrowth should be prevented.	Fluidity and interpenetration: the acceptance of growth; no single, final design; latitude for experiment and unpredictable change. A spatial plan can at best provide sound communication and transportation systems, a system of public spaces and community facilities, and a modular-type framework within which further development can proceed.

Figure 5

Distinguishing characteristics of the unitary and adaptive approaches to metropolitan planning

vantage of highlighting the essence of each, but runs the risk of casting each in such form that its supporters would probably reject the uncompromising statements.

Within our previously presented framework for dealing with metropolitan structure, the unitary approach focuses more heavily on the formal aspects (plane *I* in Figure 3, page 36) and the adaptive approach mainly on the processual aspects (plane *II*). More specifically, the unitary approach has as its major purpose the shaping of the physical environment; at the metropolitan scale the emphasis is on the spatial pattern created and preserved by the physical environment (hence, cell *I-3B* in Figure 3). The unitary approach is also concerned with the physical environment at less than metropolitan spatial scale (*I-3A*) and with the spatial pattern by which activities are distributed within the metropolis (*I-2B*). Conceptual links with the processual aspects of structure may readily be established either at the functional organizational level (between *I-2B* and *II-2B*) or at the physical environmental level (between *I-3B* and *II-3B*). Following from our reasoning in the previous sections, it would seem helpful to think of a double transition—from formal to processual (*I-2B —II-2B*) and from spatial to aspatial (*II-2B—II-2A*)—taking place as phases of the functional organization of urban life. Melvin Webber in his essay suggests the case for the logic of a transition at the physical environmental level (*I-3B—II-3B*). This places emphasis on the movement of persons, messages and goods as processual phases of the physical environment, contrasting them to the linkage of functional interdependence as processual phases of functional organization.

The adaptive approach is primarily concerned with the functioning of the metropolis, the metropolis' economy and social organization, and the formulation of decisions with respect to such organization and functioning. Within the previous framework, the focus is on processual aspects of functional organization (*II-2A* and *II-2B* in Figure 3). While much of the change is initiated in, and hence our attention is inevitably attracted to, the aspatial aspects (*II-2A*), it is a distinctive feature of metropolitan areas that changes in transportation and communication technology and shifting patterns of accessibility and locational advantage (originating in *II-2B* and *II-3B*) feed back to and must be taken into account in the organization of activities, aspatially conceived (*II-2A*). The recognition of physical environment and spatial form (as in *I-3B*) is but one aspect—that of capital investment and long-range public commitment—conceived as accommodating changes in functional organization. Transitions between processual and formal and between spatial and aspatial must be dealt with, as discussed at the close of the preceding paragraph.

Each of these unitary and adaptive approaches reflects its own value emphases and configurations. The unitary approach reflects the value placed on consensus and the conviction that agreement can be reached and, indeed, that some decisions deserve to be deliberately shaped as an entire consistent, balanced, and purposeful package. In a design sense, the unitary approach inevitably relies heavily on intuition, and represents a synthesis. It reflects a predetermination to see things whole and to create a whole design. It reflects, too, a willingness to treat communities and planning units as independent, separable, units.[21] This approach assumes and depends upon a single governmental unit or a confederation of governments such that a single approval may be achieved. Thus, importantly, this approach reflects and reinforces a political process geared to reaching consensus. It pursues the outlook that consensus is a major basis for community solidarity (drawing from an important series of concepts in social theory by Durkheim, Toennies, and others).[22] It depends upon the coalition of a potentially dominant political leader or party

and a strong designer. Going back in history, we may point to
the prince or the king and his commissioning of an architect
or an engineer to design and execute an urban development.
For a more contemporary example, we may think of the
British government commissioning Patrick Abercrombie to
prepare the Greater London Plan.[23]

The adaptive approach relies essentially not on consensus,
decree, or design imposed from the top or the outside so
much as on the interaction of many persons, firms, and governmental units in the natural interdependence that arises
with the division of labor and the complex specialization and
interchange of effort. The reliance is on pluralism of governmental actions, on highly decentralized decisions by investors,
producers, and buyers, and on the faith that the public interest will best be served by the resultant series of actions that
reflect the interests and counterinterests of the many parties
affected by, and reacting to, impending developments. While
this approach has had theoretical support in utilitarianism,
such belief in a laissez-faire framework has of course been
superseded by the realization that a decentralized, market-
place type of mechanism for reaching decisions may have
serious imperfections, and that positive governmental leadership is required to guarantee the public interest. Practically,
the adaptive approach reflects a fascinating combination of
pragmatic, administrative, and problem-solving attacks seeking to resolve issues as they arise and a social scientific interest in a better understanding of the likely consequences of
proposed policies. It is inclined to be analytic, seeking to
break down situations to their constituent parts, and empirical, searching for evidence from observed cases. Congenial to
this approach is a preponderant attention to the organization
and the interaction that results from specialization of function
and to the ways in which functional integration contributes to
community solidarity. If consensus represents a solidarity

based on likeness, functional integration represents a solidarity that emerges from difference.[24] The adaptive approach sees the contemporary metropolitan area as a favorable setting for facilitating functional integration. It assumes that much of the future is at best unknowable and that a process of enlightened adaptation is our best hope. The most persuaded proponents of this approach tend to be either unconcerned about the preparation of a single plan or policy bundle or convinced that such a plan might prove downright dysfunctional.

Urban Planning: A Résumé of Trends and Influences

During the period from World War I to the present, critically formative years for city planning in the United States, the unitary approach has generally been more dominant. This has reflected a design-oriented approach contributed by men whose main professional backgrounds were landscape architecture, architecture, or civil engineering. Strongly influential was an ideological heritage from town planning of a European vintage, in which city planning has been virtually a subfield of architecture. It is largely out of this tradition that we find utopian, spatial organizational philosophies whereby metropolitan areas might be designed. The regional city idea— proposing a series of distinguishable centers, each with a distinctive specialty and yet readily accessible to each other— was proposed by Clarence Stein, G. Holmes Perkins, and others. LeCorbusier dramatically urged a highly compact, very high-density core. Frank Lloyd Wright formulated and publicized the idea of an extremely low-density "Broadacre City." Rasmussen and other Danish town planners developed the metropolitan finger plan for Copenhagen.[25] The new town concept, although introduced by the garden-city movement, won strong support in Great Britain as a basis for metropolitan design.

The encouragement of a unitary approach was furthered by the legislative and organizational recommendations put forward by various able civic leaders and lawyers who, in their statesmanship, found congenial the "master plan" vehicle for crystallizing strong positive policy. Their recommendation that the planning agency be somewhat separated from the main flow of political decisions has, by and large, reinforced the sense of unitary recommendation expected from it.[26] The Standard Act of 1928 is a case in point.

In the decade following World War II there emerged an exploration of and support for the concept of a "general plan," spearheading renewed emphasis on a unitary approach. The general plan found itself among other variants, such as the master plan, the comprehensive plan, etc., but was distinguished for its stress on over-all policy guidance of urban physical growth and spatial arrangement. The general plan typically comprises a verbal statement of goals, assumptions, and principles and a graphic two-dimensional design showing proposed spatial arrangement. Since the general plan focuses on the character and location of major centers, the primary transportation network, and gross patterns of land use and open spaces, it is eminently adapted to metropolitan-level planning. We have already had several metropolitan general plans in the United States, and we may expect more to follow. Recent examples include those for Detroit, Atlanta, the San Francisco Bay Area, and Washington, D.C.

Supporting the unitary basis for community organization are various approaches in fields related to city planning: some political science viewpoints, scattered contributions by social philosophers and by community action leaders and other scholars, as well as the conceptions held by design professionals.[27] While there is no single homogeneous position among these representatives, they are bound loosely together by the conviction that a community can be conceived and hence planned for as a whole unit, and that it is the challenge of planning to renew a sense of "community unity."

The most pervasive earlier support for the adaptive approach within city planning came from the proponents of economic planning, public administration, and management planning. The Great Depression triggered much more thought about the need for and the possible character of economic planning than ever before.[28] While national economic planning was initiated, analogous support for regional planning was forthcoming. Political scientists and scholars of public administration also came to show an increasing, although numerically limited, interest in planning, as exemplified by the highly influential book, *The Planning Function in Urban Government,* by Robert Walker.[29] The search, here, was for the type of substantively broad staff activity that could best aid top management in formulating policy. Both the economic and the management forms of planning moved far from physical planning and, in fact, tended to deride mere physical planning.

Perhaps the culminating intellectual force in support of an adaptive view of planning was the impact of the University of Chicago's planning program, underway from 1947 to 1956.[30] The faculty of that educational program were searching for a theory of planning in which planning was conceived to be generically applicable to a broad range of activities—civil government, the military, private business, etc. While this program was not able to continue, its influence carries on, through various former staff members and students.

Supporting the adaptive view of community organization, too, are most economists and land economists, many public administrators and scholars in that field, and those political scientists and sociologists who pursue interest-group approaches. These social scientists generally lack training for thinking about spatial organization and are virtually never called upon to commit themselves to proposals for over-all spatial design. Typical of the land economist is an interest in the means for analyzing the optimum location for a specified firm (or type of firm), given a series of facts or assumptions about the context within which the firm will operate. The public administrator usually thinks in aspatial, management terms—concerned as he is with budget decisions, personnel standards, fiscal implications, etc.

In the fifteen years since World War II, partly growing out of certain approaches developed to meet difficult strategic problems during the war, the adaptive viewpoint has received important support from a series of emerging fields: operation research, systems engineering, and a variety of inter-connected developments in mathematics, statistics, and engineering. Central to these approaches has been the application of powerful new mathematical and statistical tools of analysis that have encouraged and in turn been abetted by the creation and availability of large-capacity computers and a supporting technology. Men and methods are available, and while their efforts have tended to be directed to problems of war, the national economy, business management, etc., it is clear that these approaches may prove applicable to the study of metropolitan problems. Highly competent researchers are already being drawn into a more active involvement with analysis of the metropolitan area.

Examples of this application are to be found in the large metropolitan transportation studies that have been or are currently being undertaken—for Detroit, Chicago, San Francisco, Washington, Pittsburgh, and Philadelphia, to provide a partial listing.[31] Various modes of economic analysis are also being applied to the study of metropolitan areas, starting with the economic base studies and moving to input-output or other methods. The recent New York Metropolitan Region Study provides an important example. The activity of the

Regional Science Association and the emergence of relatively new theory frameworks for the analysis of large metropolitan regions deserve to be cited. We appear to be moving into a period when urban, metropolitan, and regional economics will become important subfields of economics. These approaches are striving for explanations of metropolitan development, and are not stopping with mere descriptive summarization of trends.

A clear appraisal of the present situation indicates that the adaptive viewpoint is being vigorously championed, and that it will be particularly influential in shaping future metropolitan planning. In our view, it would be unfortunate if it were to become independently influential; just as it would be an unsatisfactory situation if the unitary view were to remain dominant. We shall deal with this question of balance between these approaches in our final section.

What Metropolitan Spatial Organization?

In accord with the unitary approach, as we have suggested, great stress is placed on the spatial form of the physical metropolis. It is expected that the planning effort will culminate in a graphic plan depicting a desirable future spatial form toward which it is recommended that community development be directed. This physical metropolis is recognized as a visual metropolis, and effort is directed toward creating an improved visual environment. The plan itself is also susceptible to visual review and may be conceived as something of a work of art in its own right. Various aesthetic principles and concepts are recognized as applicable both to the plan and to the final physical environment implied by the plan.

Up to the present at least, focality and articulation have been dominant ideas. It is usually held that a community should have a clear center (and possibly, although not inevitably, a set of subcenters); it should have distinguishable outer limits; it should have its major functional areas articulated; and it should have a reinforcing circulation pattern. A community should be imageable, to use Lynch's term; that is, it should be so clearly organized that the typical resident can carry an accurate picture in his mind of the community's major spatial form. A stereotype of a metropolitan plan fashioned in this spirit would show a dominant central area to which major radial transportation routes led but through which major surface transportation did not unduly cut; articulated residential communities, in turn broken down into neighborhoods; industrial districts carefully bounded and, if necessary, buffered; outlying commercial centers tied in with the transportation network and centered, if possible, in major communities or sectors; and, at the outer bounds of the urbanized areas, a greenbelt, clearly marking the break between city and country and controlling lateral expansion.

Ideally, the metropolitan community and its constituent communities and subcommunities would, respectively, be matched by corporate governmental units. This is, in fact, seldom the case. Congruent with the unitary approach the political organization of the metropolis could be somewhat simplified and local political units could be brought to coincide territorially with the communities designated by the plan. Also implicit in the unitary approach is the idea that creating clearly designated physical communities will help to bring about social communities at this scale and with these boundaries.

The plan prepared in the spirit of the unitary viewpoint is perhaps most applicable to those situations in which extensive and uncontrolled growth does not have to be accommodated. The conditions under which a Greater London Plan came into existence provide a case in point. Some unitary plans may connote a sense of optimum size, with excess growth accommodated in planned new towns or by other arrangements.

The adaptive approach, on the other hand, views the spatial structure of the metropolis much more as a resultant of many and varied forces than as something to be designed and worked toward for itself. Being more geared to the recognition of change and growth, it expects that changes in the spatial pattern will continually be evolving. In this light, a physical plan is seen rather as a technical necessity preparatory to capital improvements. It is not viewed as something that necessarily reduces all the elements to one single general plan; there might be a highway plan, a recreation plan, a civic center plan, etc., with integration between these plans subject to variation. Neither is a plan treated as indicating ultimate development. In short, no major synthesizing and policy-establishing role is necessarily given to *a* metropolitan plan.

Major interest is in the workings of the economic and political forces and mechanisms, rather than on the pattern of the physical environment. Even though the physically built-up city comes to a gradual outer limit or because neighborhood units are delineated, the proponent of the adaptive approach does not conceive of articulated physical boundaries accurately characterizing current or future spatial interaction patterns. He would incline toward the view that those with a unitary outlook are, unwittingly, guilty of physical environmental determinism—of assuming a greater and a more direct impact of the physical environment on social and economic life than is warranted.

If focality and articulation characterize the unitary aesthetic, than afocality, flexibility, and interpenetration would seem to be valid concepts reflecting an adaptive, interactional view of the metropolis. It may appear that proponents of the adaptive view are outwardly little concerned about the aesthetic that is implied by their approach, but this is not necessarily so. Since, from the adaptive outlook, *a* plan is not necessarily thought to be important no explicit visual aesthetic has emerged. Implicitly, however, much of the recent trend of urban and metropolitan development strongly suggests a changing spatial organization and, inevitably, a changing aesthetic. Thus we witness the great reliance on automobiles, the deterioration of fixed-rail passenger transport, the heavy emphasis on the single-family house, the complex spatial patterns of commuting, the dispersion of work places, etc. Inroads are being made on many of the main features advocated in the spirit of the traditional unitary viewpoint. It is less clear whether a positive alternative aesthetic congruent with the adaptive approach will be forthcoming.[32]

The character and impact of the urban freeway illustrate the possibilities for an adaptive aesthetic. The freeway does not necessarily have a focus (although insofar as freeways within metropolitan areas have been radial toward the metropolitan center they have to a degree reinforced a focal aesthetic). The freeway system connotes process and flow. It facilitates the ready interpenetration between city and country and between districts within the metropolis. It suggests an adaptability with which the freeway can be initially located, and much of metropolitan freeway siting carries a distinctly surgical character. Once built, it encourages a new kind of flexibility, particularly as we begin to see its potentials for mass transit. The case has been made, for example, for bus systems that make full use of freeways, as preferable to new fixed-rail transit schemes, on the grounds that their routing can be far more flexible. Certain lanes at peak hours could be assigned to buses exclusively, if necessary, while available for general use during other periods.

The Potential Integration of the Two Approaches

Having stressed the differences between these two approaches—the unitary and the adaptive—we do not intend to suggest irreconcilable conflict that will only be resolved when one camp or the other wins a fight to the finish. Indeed, the form in which we cast the approaches as ideal types has contributed to their seeming oppositeness. The two approaches contain important elements of compatibility and complementarity, and metropolitan planning will benefit by taking both into account.

The main weakness of the unitary approach is an insufficient depth of interest in and understanding of the processual and functional organizational aspects of metropolitan structure. The proponents of the unitary approach have sought, often creatively, to propose spatial arrangements of the physical environment toward which communities were to be guided by governmentally imposed implementation measures.

The main weakness of the adaptive approach is an insufficient concern for the importance of an over-all policy framework and corresponding plan proposing future spatial arrangement of the community. The interest of the advocates of this approach has been in the functional locational adjustment of the individual firm or governmental agency and in the market process for allocating favored locations.

We propose an approach to metropolitan planning that would center on the social, political and economic organization of the metropolitan community and its constituent parts. It would insist on full and first-priority treatment of the metropolis as a functioning system complete with various subsystems. It would then also deal with the optimal spatial arrangements under which these functional subsystems can operate most effectively. Out of this concern would come, first of all, policies for guiding the character and spatial patterning of the organization of the metropolis. Then flowing from this and feeding back certain opportunities and restraints would be a development policy and a spatial plan for the physical base of the metropolis.[33]

Such a focus on the organization of the metropolitan community provides the very sort of intermediate and central ground depicted in the conceptual framework presented in the first section (especially Figures 1 and 3). It forces adequate attention to the dynamic, growth-provoking organizational aspects of metropolitan life, bridging between values and physical environment and between aspatial and spatial conceptions of the community. It encourages the planner to face up to the hard realities of how urban activities and urban life are to be carried out rather than tempting him to fixate on overly general values and goals.

The objection may be raised that to focus on organization combines emphasis on bureaucratic and calculating outlooks. True, one's treatment of organization can be cold and theoretical. The planner may feel impelled to insert a humanitarian touch, bringing back a concern for personal behavior and reaction. The humanitarian will argue that the city must be rescued from organization men and from those who would see it as a monstrous system. Our reaction is that a focus on organization is not necessarily so inhuman or so insensitive to human values and interests. A broad-gauged view of organization includes living patterns and may take into account personal habits and attitudes. Inevitably, too, an organizational view will emphasize the major relationships. An essential characteristic of "organization" is that it involves the allocation of functions aspatially and the allocation of locations spatially. And while it can be fruitfully viewed for certain purposes abstractly, it also shades down into the specifics of a particular organization for a particular place, time, and purpose.

A logical starting point in the study of metropolitan organization is the proposal of a political organization for ensuring that social and economic goals are classified, determined, and carried out in accordance with an agreed-upon political decision-making process. That goals may not be readily reducible to a simple and consistent set should be understood. If a consensus on goals could be that readily achieved, we could dispense with an intricate political system for resolving conflict and difference.

With the continuing ideological preference for the small community, so that separate suburban communities appear to be politically more desirable than a single metropolitan government, we find the scales tipped toward a traditional view of lower-level local government.[34] The governmental organization of the large metropolitan area reflects the traditional grass-roots ideal more nearly than a rationally resolved level of metropolitan government dividing responsibilities with lower-level governments. The problem is one of organization, how a set of governments can be put together with appropriate functions clearly allocated to each. We still need the strictly local units that encourage political participation and citizen identification; we also need a well equipped metropolitan government eager to tackle problems most appropriately handled at the metropolitan level.

Each metropolitan community faces important social-policy issues. In the broadest sense the community must organize itself to try to determine its future. It must determine policies regarding housing, the character of residential districts, the distribution of workplaces in relation to residences, and the creation and preservation of the main business centers. A major current issue regarding racial integration raises questions of whether previously segregated minority residents are to be welcomed in all sections of the metropolis. The question of whether the growth of the largest metropolitan areas will be encouraged or discouraged also calls for social policy.

The metropolitan community also faces questions as to how it shall develop economically. We still tend to carry an ideology of letting business develop as it will, although in reality various governmental units in many ways influence the course of the economy. The hard questions are how various real or potential governmental actions or policies will affect the economy and its different segments. The distribution of economic activities among the separate local governmental units within the metropolitan area is of great significance, for it affects the respective tax bases, may help to trigger further economic growth, and, through the locational pattern of employment opportunities, affects residential development.

Each of these aspects of metropolitan organization—political, social and economic—carries over into related spatial organizational questions and alternatives.[35] But, basically, we would submit that the spatial organizational riddles cannot be meaningfully resolved until there is reasonably clear understanding of what it is that is to be distributed in space. Then the critical question is what the relative impacts of alternative policies or plans will be on the well-being of residents and of the systems making up the city.

Specifically, we must grant the logic of preparing a plan (or, if preferred, a certain number of alternative plans). It is only by so doing that the possible congruence or conflict between land users can be explored. But how ensure that the plan will be more than a matter of form? How does such a plan get fully tied to the processes by which the metropolis functions? How can we depict the functional organization of the metropolis and the implications of alternative spatial arrangements on this functional organization?

We are in urgent need of methods for describing and analyzing how the large city functions as a system, and how smaller systems fit into the over-all system. An important part of planning would then be to determine how this system and its parts can best function. Only then can the task of recommending an appropriate physical environment as a base be meaningfully tackled.

NOTES

[1] Kevin Lynch and Lloyd Rodwin have set as a criterion for urban-form analysis that the form be "significant at the city or metropolitan scale, that is, [have qualities] which can be controlled at that scale and which also have different effects when arranged in different patterns that are describable at that scale. This criterion excludes, without in any way denying their importance, such features as intercity spacing (describable only beyond the city level) or the relation of the front door of a house to the street (which is hard to describe on the city scale unless uniform, difficult to control at that level, and whose city-wide pattern of distribution would seem to be of no importance)." Lynch and Rodwin, "A Theory of Urban Form," *Journal of the American Institute of Planners,* XXIV (1958), 203.

[2] A somewhat similar hypothesis was developed and tested in one study of a housing project by Leon Festinger, Stanley Schachter, and Kurt Back, reported in *Social Pressures in Informal Groups: A Study of Human Factors in Housing* (New York: Harper and Brothers, 1950), pp. 35 ff.

[3] Also examined in much this form by Festinger and his colleagues, *ibid.*

[4] Gideon Sjoberg, for example, has suggested: "It is questionable procedure . . . to assume any direct correspondence between values and the social or ecological structure of urban centers." See his essay, "Comparative Urban Sociology," in Robert K. Merton, Leonard Broom, Leonard S. Cottrell, Jr. (eds.), *Sociology Today: Problems and Prospects* (New York: Basic Books, 1959), p. 346.

[5] Robert B. Mitchell and Chester Rapkin, *Urban Traffic: A Function of Land Use* (New York: Columbia University Press, 1954); John Rannells, *The Core of the City: A Pilot Study of Changing Land Uses in Central Business Districts* (New York: Columbia University Press, 1956); and, published after the first draft of this essay had been completed, Robert B. Mitchell, "The New Frontier in Metropolitan Planning," *Journal of the American Institute of Planners,* XXVII (August, 1961), 169-175.

[6] Rannells, *op. cit.,* p. 13.

[7] This phrase is also the title of chapter 3, pp. 33-59, *op. cit.,* in which the essential phases of the study which concern us are to be found.

[8] A. Benjamin Handler, "What is Planning Theory?" *Journal of the American Institute of Planners,* XXIII (1957), 144-150, particularly pp. 147-150.

[9] *Ibid.,* p. 149.

[10] Lynch and Rodwin, *op. cit.;* Lynch, "The Pattern of the Metropolis," in Rodwin and Lynch (eds.), "The Future Metropolis," *Daedalus*, XC (Winter, 1961), 79-98; Lynch, *The Image of the City* (Cambridge: The Technology Press and Harvard University Press, 1960); Lynch, "A Classification System for the Analysis of the Urban Pattern" (Mimeographed, April, 1961).

[11] *Journal of the American Institute of Planners*, XXVI (May, 1960), 104-109.

[12] Guttenberg in another article has dealt very clearly with the subtle distinctions between physical facilities and activities. "A Multiple Land Use Classification System," *Journal of the American Institute of Planners*, XXV (August, 1959), 143-150.

[13] We shall not try to list all of the volumes here. Two that are relevant in exploring in detail the nature and likely future of specific activities that have always been important for New York are Roy B. Helfgott *et al., Made in New York,* and Sidney M. Robbins and Nestor E. Terleckyj, *Money Metropolis* (both Cambridge: Harvard University Press, 1960).

[14] Britton Harris, "Plan or Projection: An Examination of the Use of Models in Planning," *Journal of the American Institute of Planners*, XXVI (November, 1960), 265-272; Harris, "Some Problems in the Theory of Intra-Urban Location" (Mimeographed, April, 1961).

[15] Lowdon Wingo, Jr., *Transportation and Urban Land* (Washington, D.C.: Resources for the Future, Inc., 1961).

[16] Melvin M. Webber, "Transportation Planning Models," *Traffic Quarterly*, XV (July, 1961), 373-390.

[17] As Harris puts it, this attempt via behavioral models to explain the nature of metropolitan development is process-oriented. "Being process-oriented it is almost inevitably forced to consider the events which lead to growth and change in the urban framework. These events are the results of actions by decision-makers, although frequently it is both practical and attractive to deal with aggregates of decision-makers rather than with individual units." "Some Problems in the Theory of Intra-Urban Location," p. 6.

[18] Parsons has, for example, suggested three main and clearly distinguishable systems: the cultural (and our *1A* and *1B* cells correspond), the social (and our *2A* and *2B* are in this spirit, if not similarly defined), and the personality (for which we have no counterpart). Talcott Parsons and Edward A. Shils, (eds.), *Toward a General Theory of Action* (Cambridge: Harvard University Press, 1951), esp. pp. 6-8, 110-233.

[19] As Mitchell has stated: "Most planning today is static. It portrays a desired urban pattern at some future date." *Op. cit.,* p. 171.

[20] I am particularly indebted to Melvin M. Webber for ideas in preparing part of Figure 5. Also helpful was a graduate student report prepared under his direction, *Studies in Metropolitan Planning* (Berkeley: University of California, Department of City and Regional Planning, January 1960, mimeographed).

[21] I am indebted to Melvin M. Webber for this idea that the unitary view may see the world as composed of independent units, reflecting earlier approaches in biology and physics. He suggests that more recent develop-

ments favor a stress on the interconnectedness of units within a more broadly viewed system.

[22] See particularly Emile Durkheim, *The Division of Labor in Society* (originally written 1893, translated by George Simpson, 1933; Glencoe, Ill.: The Free Press, 1947); Charles P. Loomis' translation of Ferdinand Toennies, *Fundamental Concepts of Sociology* (New York: American Book Company, 1940); Ronald Freedman *et al.*, *Principles of Sociology* (New York: Henry Holt, 1952), chaps. 4 and 5; Martin Meyerson and Edward Banfield, *Politics, Planning and the Public Interest* (Glencoe, Ill.: The Free Press, 1955), esp. pp. 322-329.

[23] This is developed more fully in Donald L. Foley, *Controlling London's Growth: Planning the Great Wen 1940-1960* (Berkeley and Los Angeles: University of California Press, 1963).

[24] See the references cited in previous footnote.

[25] See Catherine Bauer's full discussion of major design alternatives in her "First Job: Control New-City Sprawl," *Architectural Forum*, CV (September, 1956), 105-112. See also Steen Eiler Rasmussen, *Greater Copenhagen Planning* (Copenhagen: Ejnar Munksgaard, Ltd., 1952).

[26] See Robert C. Hoover's discussion, "On Master Plans and Constitutions," *Journal of the American Institute of Planners*, XXVI (February, 1960), esp. p. 10.

[27] In viewing the community as a governmental unit, the political scientist comes to hold a unitary view. He sees sharp boundaries, for administrative purposes. He senses a "public" interest on government's part. Lewis Mumford and other social philosophers have explored the community concept, and urge a rediscovery of community in an essentially unitary sense.

[28] Illustrative of this was the evolution of Wesley Mitchell's thought. See Forest G. Hill, "Wesley Mitchell's Theory of Planning," *Political Science Quarterly*, LXXII (March, 1957), 100-118.

[29] First published 1940. 2nd edition; Chicago: University of Chicago Press, 1950.

[30] Harvey S. Perloff, *Education for Planning* (Baltimore: Johns Hopkins Press, 1957), part III.

[31] For one of the most promising examples, see Penn-Jersey Transportation Study, *Prospectus* (1959).

[32] See, however, Jesse Reichek, "On the Design of Cities," *Journal of the American Institute of Planners*, XXVII (May, 1961), 141-143.

[33] Robert B. Mitchell's recent proposal for a "land use plan" for "the distribution and intensity of land users and their activities," to be followed, perhaps later and in greater detail, by a "land improvements plan" to "provide for the adaptation of the physical structure of the area to the needs and requirements imposed by land use change" is very much in this same spirit. His interest in process, in this recent paper, focuses mainly on the developmental process by which a metropolitan area changes over time, while my concern with process is limited more specifically to day-to-day interaction processes within the metropolitan area. *Op. cit.*, pp. 172-175.

[34] Cf. Robert C. Wood, *Suburbia: Its People and Their Politics* (Boston: Houghton Mifflin Company, 1958).

[35] For as Wingo and Perloff have suggested, a metropolitan government must push itself to some "broad commitment to certain long-range characteristics of the city's form and organization which are implicit in its objectives." Lowdon Wingo, Jr., and Harvey S. Perloff, "The Washington Transportation Plan: Technics or Politics," *Regional Science Association Papers and Proceedings*, VII (1961), 249-262.

The Urban Place and the Nonplace Urban Realm

Melvin M. Webber

*Indeed the whole notion that one is always in some defi-
nite "place" is due to the fortunate immobility of most of
the large objects on the earth's surface. The idea of
"place" is only a rough practical approximation: there is
nothing logically necessary about it, and it cannot be made
precise.*

BERTRAND RUSSELL

I. CONCEPTIONS OF THE URBAN PLACE

In the recent flurry of commentaries on the variously
alleged trends and implications of metropolitan growth, there
has been little basis for agreement or disagreement among
the commentators, even about the nature of the phenomenon
under discussion. This is scarcely surprising, for each group
of observers views the metropolitan communities through the
colored glasses of its own discipline or profession, and each
sees something different from what others see. Their observations may bore, or perplex, or fascinate others; but they are
not easily fitted into the others' conceptual systems.

If the experience of interdisciplinary inquiry on other matters is relevant here, we may be confident that we need a

simplified and organizing concept and a common language that, initially, can synoptically treat just the few paramount dimensions of the phenomenon being observed. This need is especially apparent in metropolitan planning. In its early years it is tending to mirror city planning's emphasis upon certain small-scale, static, locational, and physical aspects of urbanization. But as it evolves, we can expect the emergence of a macroscopic frame of reference that applies uniquely to the large dimensions of urban development rather than to the small parts. And even more to be hoped for, as a political, welfare-oriented activity, it may identify and deal with those critical processes of the spatial urban community that directly affect the quintessential qualities of urban life.

This essay reflects an attempt to contribute to a conception of urban communities that may have utility in metropolitan policy making. It is oriented to metropolitan *processes* (a verb view) for which it seeks to identify the matching spatial *form* (a noun view), and hence it seeks to pose a dynamic portrait of metropolitan *form in action* (a gerund view).

By focusing upon functional interdependencies—upon linkages expressed as interactions—I mean to deal with urban communities as *functional processes*. By tracing the spatial configurations of communication and transportation channels, buildings, and activities, I mean to deal with the processual correlates as a *structural form* phenomenon—as a static arrangement. By dealing with process and form simultaneously, I am looking for a clearer conception of the urban communities as *spatially structured processes*.[1]

At the heart of structured urban processes in social intercourse—the business transactions, the exchanges of information, the intricately complex webs of interactions—through which urbanites deal with each other and by which they satisfy the interdependencies upon which their livelihoods and their welfare depend. Much of this interaction occurs at the expanding urban places, but, increasingly, interaction transcends the places at which people live. Those who share in this spatially dispersed communication are in some degree participants in urban communities that are of a *non*-nodal sort—urban communities having spatial forms that are vastly more dispersed than we have been ready to recognize.

To see this we shall have to don a special set of glasses; but before doing so in Section III, let us first attempt to see the city as it is traditionally viewed and then, in Section II, try to clarify our language and systematize our measurements of the traditional city.

Conceptions of the City and Region as Places

Both in the urban sciences and in urban planning, the dominant conception of the metropolitan area and of the city sees each as a unitary place. Students who have been concerned with the spatial distribution of nodal, urban settlements have made the clearest exposition of the place idea, but the conception is probably as old as urbanization itself.[2] A settlement of whatever size is seen as a physically urbanized segment of land on which buildings and other physical equipment are closely spaced, and where people conduct activities that are typically more closely related to and dependent upon each other than they are to activities located in other settlements. Each settlement is surrounded by a nonurbanized territory in which cultivated fields, pastures, forests, or bodies of water predominate. Thus, the urban settlement—the town, the city, the metropolitan area—is a physically separate unit that is visually identifiable from the air. There are other marked nonvisual and nonphysical counterparts, of course, for the settlement is also the locus of trade, production, and human interactions of all sorts; and the inhabitants follow different styles of life from residents of "nonurban" places.

A settlement is variously called a village, town, or city, depending primarily upon its population size. Population size is measured according to certain conventions about physical separation from populations located in other settlements ("non-urbanized" land intervening), and other conventions about the legal incorporation of urban territories and about degrees of interaction. It is commonly recognized that governmental boundary lines are really inadequate bases for defining urban areas, since they are not important indicators of either the physical patterns of settlement or of the conduct of activities within settlements. But it is apparently less commonly seen that physical separation is not a necessary criterion of urbanness, either.

In the natural history of urban expansion, villages, towns, and cities have physically enlarged to fuse one with another;[3] and we have expanded our taxonomy accordingly to include the class "metropolitan area" as an equivalent, though larger, variety of settlement. Physical separation and legal boundaries are brought over as parts of the defining characteristics. And now, when the once-separated settlements of the Atlantic seaboard are themselves showing signs of physically fusing, there is an avid interest in adding a further class to the taxonomy of urban places. The debate seems not to question whether a new phenomenon is occurring, but rather who shall get to name it.

Much of the current clamor about the fusing physical pattern of urbanized land derives from the notion that a metropolitan area is a physical thing. The new urbanized area maps are being read to say that something new is happening, largely because the old maps always showed nodal, discontinuous areas of physical settlement, and the new ones show large physical agglomerations and incipient physically urbanized strips several hundred miles long. This is indeed a new scale of physical form, and it may indeed call for different approaches to facilities planning than those required by the nodal forms. But the emergence of large, physically contiguous urban forms does not necessarily reflect changes either in the functional organization of the physically fusing cities or in the organized processes operating within them. It is likely that the new scale of the physical forms reflects spatial linkage patterns that are as old as colonial America; in our limited view of the metropolitan system's surface, we may have failed to recognize that the patterns of intercourse have long extended far beyond the urban nodes.

An important elaboration of the urban-place conception, which regards the urban unit as a regional phenomenon, assigns to each place the surrounding territory with its population and activities; and the urban region is thus conceived as the node plus its hinterland.[4] A further refinement of the urban-region concept seeks to account for the variation in size and the hierarchical structure of urban settlements. In Christaller's classic formulation the area of the hinterland surrounding each settlement is conceived to be a function of the population size and kinds of activities performed in the nodal settlement.[5] As in the Copernican model of the solar system, the large numbers of small towns, each with its own hinterland, are conceived to be satellites of larger towns, which in turn are satellites of still larger towns, until the primate city dominates the entire settlement pattern. The place in the hierarchy is also a function of population size, and population size is related to the kinds of functions that are performed at the various settlements.[6] The most specialized cities serve the largest territories; the least specialized cities primarily serve the local farming areas.[7]

But irrespective of the place in the hierarchy, all the inhabitants of each place are seen as full-time participants in the communal life of that place. The activities and the people engaging in them are thought to be more closely related to others within that urban region than they are to those who inhabit other urban regions. Although it is generally recognized that the markets for some of the goods and services they produce are world-wide, the primary market for most of the local production is typically within the settlement itself and within the several hierarchically scaled levels of hinterland that sequentially surround it.

Within these places of concentrated settlement, density of resident population and density of employment have tended to be concentrically gradient, peaking up to a primate center of production, trade, and residence within each settlement. In the largest urban places, subcenters typically persist at the sites of old settlements that were once physically separated. The physical and activity components of the spatial structure of large urban places thus have typically been hierarchically organized in multinucleated and multicentered patterns. The possible future spatial forms of these nuclei and centers depend on what goes on in them; they are in some degree manipulable; and so they are of great concern to the welfare-oriented metropolitan planner. It is therefore important that we understand what goes on in central places; and what goes on is largely human interaction and the human action that makes interaction fruitful.

The City as a Communications System

The urban planners' images of the "good life" in the "good society" are somewhat diverse; their ideological and theoretical bases are also varied; but they pursue a common approach to the public interest. By changing the physical and the locational environments at the places in which families live out their lives and in which groups conduct their business, the lives and the businesses can be improved.

In part, this emphasis upon locational-physical place stems from the architectural heritage of the profession. In part, it stems from the fact that our institutions place local governments in the business of building large and influential portions of the physical environment, give them authority to guide or control certain private locational decisions, but prevent them from interfering more directly in the processes of life and business. In part, it is because most planners share a conviction that the physical and locational variables are key determinants of social and economic behavior and of social welfare.

Although there is very little that is yet clearly demonstrated about the causal relations between physical-locational environment and welfare, it is now becoming apparent that, insofar as a relation exists, one of the important links in the causal chain is the influence that spatial arrangements have upon communications.

The unique commodity that the city offers to location seekers is accessibility. Individuals and groups who locate there are usually more able to deal with other individuals and groups who are also located there than they can with those who are distant. The specialization, and hence dependency, that accompanies economic development requires that household and business establishments be in contact with an increasing variety of other establishments; the city is attractive to them primarily because it offers the economies of urbanization, which facilitate the establishment and maintenance of these contacts.[8]

The size and the degree of concentration that marks the establishment cluster within a given space bear directly upon the costs and ease of intercourse and upon the potentialities for creating new wealth. The familiar spatial clustering of business establishments in downtown districts clearly reflects the efforts of each establishment to increase its accessibility to linked establishments, to reduce the costs of overcoming the distances that separate them, and to exploit the external economies that clustering engenders. In turn, the heterogeneous mixtures of businesses and populations create opportunities for the intercultural exchanges of ideas that have made cities the traditional centers of civilization. The history of city growth, in essence, is the story of man's eager search for ease of human interaction.

Our large modern urban nodes are, in their very nature, massive communication systems. In these intricately complex switchboards, men are actively involved in the business of producing and distributing the information that is the essential stuff of civilization—the accumulated wisdom, descriptive accounts, ideas and theories, reports of human events, laws, contracts, records of transactions, gossip, and the ideational products of the arts and the sciences.

The means by which these varieties of information are transmitted are becoming more refined, as the sheer volume that must be handled rapidly increases. Face-to-face conversation remains one of the most effective for some purposes, and for this reason certain business establishments seem willing to suffer high costs of congestion in the dense business districts. Telephones, other electronic transmission devices, and the postal services offer very effective substitutes for a great deal of the person-to-person contact that would otherwise need to be conducted face to face. These are further supplemented for mass communication by radio, television, concerts, lectures, and store displays, and by newspapers, magazines, books, journals, and other printed materials. Libraries, files, and museums store important information for later use. For all these, the urban settlement, and especially the large urban settlement, offers the most effective channels, and it is therefore the major locus of communication flow. It is there that interdependent specialists of various kinds are best able to exchange information, services, and goods; and this exchange is the medium through which economic and cultural wealth are produced.

An Index of Cultural Wealth

We have become accustomed to using per capita income as an index of the relative economic well-being of populations in different places or at different times. However coarse, per capita income is a very useful indicator of economic welfare for many policy-making purposes, being roughly equivalent to volumes of goods and services consumed. But it does not directly record the large component of wealth that is not sensitively priced in the economic markets—the information that the average person receives.

Richard L. Meier has recently suggested that, as a supplement to national income accounting, a system of social accounts be established, designed to provide an index to the cultural wealth of populations by drawing upon measurements of the volume and variety of information flowing through the public communication channels.[9] It is the *public* information that is important, he rightly contends, because private communications that do not feed into the cumulating storehouse of knowledge have no cultural value, however great may be the personal values. Communication flowing through public channels can be shared and therefore can contribute to cultural development.

In primitive societies, where the accumulated volume of ideas and information is small, the volume of information flowing through the public channels is also small; and per capita levels of information received are low. In highly developed societies, the store of knowledge is large; the rates of information flow are very high; and the per capita receipts are correspondingly high. Meier's early estimates of relative levels of information receipts in San Francisco and Djakarta, for example, indicate that the average American may be receiving up to ten times as much public information as the Indonesian.[10] As literacy and cultural development in Indonesia increase, the reception rates can be expected to rise accordingly.

A system of social accounts, recording rates of information flow, might gauge the rates and levels of cultural progress for the Indonesians, and it might well provide Americans with the conceptual tool we have never had for systematically estimating our own cultural progress and for evaluating the effectiveness of various governmental programs designed to foster cultural growth. And since the city, in its nature, is a center of cultural growth—the major place at which ideas and information are produced and distributed—such an accounting system may give us a fairly sensitive means for evaluating the relative cultural wealth of different cities and of different parts of cities, and for recording changes through time. In addition, it may offer a device for evaluating the effectiveness of various plans and programs for urban spatial structure.

Most important of all, it might encourage us to see urbanity —the essence of urbanness—not as buildings, not as land use patterns, not as large, dense, and heterogeneous population aggregations, but as a quality and as a diversity of life that is distinct from and in some measure independent of these other characteristics. Urbanity is more profitably conceived as a property of the amount and the variety of one's participation in the cultural life of a world of creative specialists, of the amount and the variety of the information received. Thus, urbanity is no longer the exclusive trait of the city dweller; the suburbanite and the exurbanite are among the most urbane of men; increasingly the farmers themselves are participating in the urban life of the world.

And yet, space does intervene as a barrier against some levels of communication. Planners have long been intuitively aware of the importance that spatial arrangements of activities have for ease of communication. Presumably this is part of the rationale for the traditional focus upon land-use patterns and upon the physical facilities for transportation. But urban planning has never explicitly dealt with spatial patterns of information-flow through the urban system.

As Foley has noted in his essay above, urban planning has typically approached the city within a unitary conceptual framework. The urban settlement is seen as a place in which physical artifacts are spatially distributed and in which activity locations are geometrically arranged. Although a great deal of attention has been paid to the spatial patterns of personal trips, the dominant conception is nonetheless that of a static spatial arrangement. Neither traditional city plans nor their underlying studies have successfully depicted the city as a social process operating in space. And yet, city planners have traditionally sought to influence social processes, and particularly the processes of human interaction, by manipulating the spatial arrangements.

Endeavoring to find ways in which the pace of life might be reduced, some city planners suggest that large concentrations of people be discouraged, that small "self-contained" towns be developed, that population sizes and densities be lowered, that business centers be restricted in size. And it may be that these are urged because the ongoing rise in the levels of human interaction is viewed with alarm.

Others have viewed the expansion of nodal settlements with

approval, if not enthusiasm. City plans directed toward increasing the spatial intensity of social, economic, and political intercourse have sought to encourage locational patterns that would increase accessibility among related populations. The locational-physical design expression of this idea has been higher densities, large concentrations of people into larger settlements, higher concentrations in business centers, and transportation networks that would encourage concentration and interchange.

Whatever the ideological orientation with respect to population concentration and communication levels and whether the resulting spatial designs have sought to encourage bustling cities or tranquil towns, the plans have uniformly been expressed in other than interaction terms. Typically the plans are stated as static distributions of land-use categories, sometimes with distributions of resident populations expressed as densities. Insofar as the plans' authors have deliberately sought to influence interaction intensities, or at least insofar as they've been aware of the communications implications of their spatial designs, we may assume that they have sought to express interaction in the language of land use and density.

But difficulties arise here. However adequate the land use and density language may be for depicting static site characteristics, it is not capable of dealing explicitly and specifically with the dynamic, locational patterns of human communications that occur through space but transcend any given place.

The Shortcomings of the Land-Use and Density Concepts

As it has come to be used in city and metropolitan planning, "land use" is analytically imprecise. It refers simultaneously—and hence ambiguously—to physical land itself, including its geophysical characteristics and the flora and fauna it supports, to physical building types, and to certain characteristics of the activities that take place upon the surface of the land.

Although the distinctions are seldom clearly made in current practice, the classification of activity characteristics—that is, the *use* component—could be extracted and dealt with exclusively. In the simplest form, land-using *activities* can be classified according to the social or economic functions they represent, the acts that people perform while conducting the activities, the kinds of goods or services involved, or, possibly, according to some other system of classification.[11] The locations at which each type of activity takes place can be identified; counts can be made; and the information can be recorded in tabular, graphic, or electronic form.

As a further refinement, the variously classifiable activities conducted within each establishment can be distinguished, so that the activities that are hidden by the ownership (or establishment) unit are revealed.[12] And as a still further refinement, the data can be weighted by income, value added, dollar sales, tonnage produced, or by some other indicator of volume of activity conducted by each establishment at its site. If the volumes are shown as a ratio of the indicator to area occupied, the result is density, indicating volume of activity per unit of site space.

But even these refinements yield a static picture of activity characteristics at discrete sites. It is quite true that the compilation of all individual sites into a city-wide picture does indeed reveal something more than did the individual bits of data alone. But the macroscopic picture is still only a summation of static characteristics at individual sites. Even the most conceptually refined of land-use and density approaches can give only a variation on a snapshot picture, showing the site-locations at which activities are conducted. It is also true, of course, that a series of snapshots (a motion picture) can depict conditions at various moments in the course of time; and it is quite possible to show dynamic *changes* in the spatial patterns of activity sites. But this is nonetheless a view of static distributions at instants in time.

This will still not answer our need for a way of viewing the city as a dynamic system in action, a system in which people interact with each other through space at every instant in time.[13] The problem calls for something akin to a musical score—a recordable language capable of expressing action.

Density provides more direct clues to probable dynamic interaction intensity than does land use alone. The larger the number of people living or working in a given area, all other characteristics held constant, the higher is the level of interaction among individuals that can be expected. With any given transportation-communication system, the lower the density, the lower are the probabilities for contacts with others, and the lower the intensity and the varieties of interaction that can be expected.

But density is only part of the story. Like land use, density is a site characteristic that relates to small-scale areal units. Irrespective of how finely grained the areal statistical units might be, and despite the fact that averaging methods may be applied to create smooth density curves over large territories, a density picture is by its very nature a reflection of population and activity distribution *at discrete places*.

It is clear, of course, that a skilled city planner or a skilled urban scientist is able to read a combination of a land-use and a density map to mean dynamic relations among populations at different places, just as a skilled architect can visualize a building in use by reading the plans; but these relations are indirectly implied rather than explicitly stated. When supplemented by origin-destination information about person and goods movements, especially if further supplemented by data showing information flow through space, the picture would be considerably clearer; for these latter do specifically deal with interaction. But with the exception of travel information (very little is yet known about the spatial message-communications patterns), most city planners deal with the city with essentially static concepts; and, if we may judge by the kinds of land-use maps and plans they prepare, they tend to view the city as a static arrangement of physical objects.[14]

Our traditional emphasis has been upon the physical city, conceived as artifact; upon the spatial arrangement of activity locations, conceived as land-use pattern; and upon the urban settlement, conceived as a unitary place. We have sought to influence the forms of each of these, with the purpose of improving certain behavioral aspects of the society. Yet we have neglected the conception of the city as a social system in action.

For metropolitan planning purposes it is important that we also see the city as a culturally conditioned system of dynamic interrelationships among individuals and groups, as these are modified by their locational distributions.

Hence I am here searching for a holistic conception of the city that can analytically identify process-relations and form-relations—that can more sharply distinguish between, and thus facilitate our understanding of, the relationships among the physical patterns, the spatial activity patterns, and the spatial interaction patterns that are the expression of economic and social behavior. Our descriptive language must be capable of yielding a macroscopic, synoptic view of the metropolitan community, in which long-range goals for the larger urban system can be explicitly and clearly expressed.

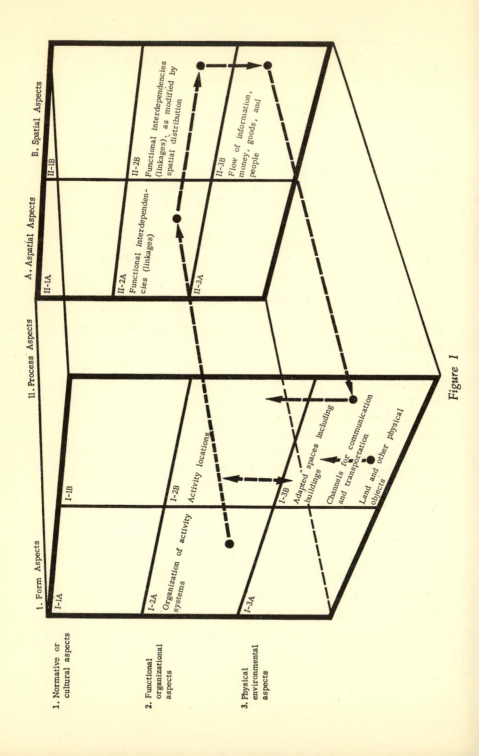

Figure 1

II. THE SPATIAL STRUCTURE TRICHOTOMY OF URBAN PLACES

The Components of Spatial Structure

Foley has identified twelve analytically distinctive aspects of metropolitan structure. It will satisfy our more limited purposes here to focus our attention on certain of the spatial aspects noted in his Figure 3 and excerpted in my Figure 1. I suggest that the metropolitan spatial planner may fruitfully view spatial structure as comprising four related, but analytically separable, components. (Identified in cells II-2B, II-3B, I-3B, and I-2B).

In this context the crucial components of over-all structure are the linkages among activity-engaged establishments which form the aspatial network of functional interdependencies (II-2A in Figure 1), as these interdependencies are then modified by spatial distributions (II-2B in Figure 1). I define linkages simply as the dependency ties that relate individuals and groups to each other.[15] Viewed aspatially, these include the ties that become reflected in input-output analysis and those that students of group dynamics have been examining. They are the invisible relations that bring the various interdependent business establishments, households, voluntary groups, and personal friends into working associations with each other—into operating systems.

The spatial distributions of individuals and groups modify the natures and strengths of their linkages, as propinquity or distance work to open or foreclose opportunities for contact. However invisible and intangible these networks of linkages are, they appear to me to be the important connections between the physical-locational environment, systems of social organization, and the cultural and economic goals that communities seek. Plans intended to influence spatial arrangements have meaning and utility for social welfare to the degree that they affect these invisible linkages in salutary ways. Linkage, conceived in the general sense, thus becomes the important basis for formulating metropolitan policies.

I know of no empirical way in which these ties could be identified and their strengths measured other than by empirically observing their manifestations. Hence I think it sufficient, at least for current metropolitan planning purposes, to limit our descriptions to overt evidences of linkages: the flows of information, money, people, and goods among establishments. I propose, therefore, that, as a minimum, metropolitan planning should deal explicitly with three of the four components of metropolitan spatial structure:

1. spatial flows of information, money, people, and goods;
2. locations of the physical channels and of the adapted spaces[16] that physically house activities; and
3. locations of activity places.

1. *The first component, then, is the flow of information, money, people, and goods through which human interactions take place.* We have already recognized that interactions among individuals and groups are the essential processes by which the business of society is transacted, and that they take many forms. A large volume of interaction occurs among people who are spatially separated and who interact through the various electrical and mechanical communication channels. Some interaction requires that the communicators be in the same place, and these may therefore also involve the movement of persons to a common meeting place; other interaction is satisfied by the movement of goods from one place to another. In a literal sense, all these involve physical movement through physical channels.

By measuring the volumes of information, money, persons, and goods flow, and by recording origins, destinations, and routes, we should be better equipped to understand the functional interdependencies among industries or, if the data were sufficiently detailed, among establishments. We should also be better equipped to describe the processes by which these linkages are maintained through space. Such measurements may also be made to yield efficiency indices of alternative spatial arrangements. For example, expressed as units of information, the *varieties* of activity-related interactions occurring at a given urban space may be taken as an indication of the richness of the cultural and economic life of the people occupying that space. The quantity of information flowing within a given space may be taken as an indicator of probable levels of cultural productivity. Together, variety and quantity of information may yield an index to those elusive qualities of city life that have been intuitively attached to the term "urbanity." [17]

Planners have frequently contended that the number of miles traveled per capita is an indication of the relative efficiency of the spatial arrangement, the postulate being that travel per se is an unproductive activity.[18] A more sensitive index might be constructed comparing the effectiveness of the communications system in permitting messages to be substituted for persons—or goods—movements.[19] These and other measures might be employed to evaluate the effectiveness with which the metropolitan processes would work under conditions imposed by different metropolitan forms.

2. *The second component of spatial structure comprises the spatial form of the communication and transportation channel networks; of the adapted spaces, including physical buildings; and of the landscape and other physical objects. The spatial arrangement of the networks and the capacities*

of their channels bear strong influence upon the ease with which interactions can take place and, hence, upon the locations at which activities are conducted. For any individual establishment, the arrangements of adapted spaces, including buildings of various types, and the possibilities for constructing new buildings in various places similarly establish limits upon locational choice; for establishments in the aggregate, they establish limits on the over-all spatial patterns of activity distribution. The influences of topographic and other landscape features are apparent.

Some of the relations between channel capacity and activity locations have been understood for a long time. Land developers and city planners have traditionally designed transportation facilities with the express intention of affecting accessibility relationships and thereby influencing activity locations. The most dramatic deliberate effort was successfully carried out by the Western railroads; but the extensions of suburban streetcar lines and the construction of intra-urban subway lines and freeways are of quite the same sort. Less deliberate, no doubt, but equally effective were the expansions of telephone and mail systems and the recent development of the airlines. Each has made possible and, in a limited sense, has caused the expansion of Western metropolitan settlements on a scale that could not otherwise have occurred.

Where channel capacities are inadequate to the communication or transportation loads and when relief is not in sight, locational adjustments inevitably follow. Accommodations to peak-hour highway congestion are the most familiar, but similar locational adjustments to inadequacies of electricity, water, fuel, rail, and shipping channels are common. The capacities of channels for message-sending have proved to be remarkably elastic, with only infrequent congestion occurring. The telephone and mail systems have been successful in absorbing great increases in traffic loads by vastly increasing the number of messages that can be simultaneously transmitted in a given channel and by expanding a very fine-grained intra- and interuban network. They thus approximate free access from any location and greatly widen the range of locational choice.[20]

The channels for face-to-face communications are of a different sort from any of the others. They comprise the meeting places—convention halls, restaurants, lecture rooms, offices, street corners, stock exchanges, living rooms, and so on —where communicators can occupy a common space. These "channels" are simultaneously the buildings and groups of buildings that house activities of various kinds, as well as the streets on which they face. The central business districts of large cities are, in this sense, large communication channels. Businessmen who rely upon rapid access to accurate information have traditionally chosen to locate there precisely because information received on a face-to-face basis tends to be accorded the greatest credence, and they have therefore sought a tap into the channel. The probabilities of making chance face-to-face contacts are greatest where the density of men sharing similar interests is greatest, and this fact largely accounts for the scale and the vitality of a Wall Street or a Seventh Avenue garment mart.

The other major part of the physical form comprises the buildings and other adapted spaces.[21] Their styles, sizes, heights, spatial patterns, and the spacing between them contribute to the visual scene of the city, forming the picture that a camera records. The important attribute, of course, is the degree of conformity to the functional requirements of the activities that the occupants perform. But buildings are important also because their inherent permanence exerts a strong constraint on locational choice.

We are all too aware of the limitations that a stock of old housing has upon the lower-income families' spatial patterns. We are frequently reminded of the incubator function of the old lofts, and of the permissive role that old store buildings have for the survival of the small merchant. At any moment in time, the existing stock of buildings and utility lines exerts a dead weight on the possibilities for changes in physical form, for the imbedded investment is tremendous.[22] Thus, changes in activity locations are not easily made, since certain types of activity are most efficiently performed in buildings of certain types. Of course there is not a one-to-one relation, and some buildings have been used for every class of activity that shows up on the typical land-use map. But families do prefer to live in houses, and manufacturers do prefer buildings designed as factories.

The pace of change in the organization for economic and social activities is very rapid. Whole new industries are rising within the course of but a few years. New linkage patterns are being created, inducing new communication patterns and calling for different spatial arrangements of activity places than previously existed. The inherent stability of the physical plant of the city imposes a restriction on the possibilities for change, however.

Architects and architecturally oriented metropolitan planners are prone to regard the physical plant of the metropolis as an end in itself, since its visual qualities are so apparent to all who use the metropolis. I would contend, on the other hand, that the paramount function of the physical plant is to accommodate the kinds of activities performed there and to accommodate the interactions among individuals and groups who conduct those activities. The physically well-designed metropolis is one having a spatial arrangement of channels and adapted spaces that facilitates the individual users' interactions and locations. Matched to the networks of linkages and to the systems of activities, the well-designed physical plant is integral to the total economic-cultural-political system, and it should be as flexibly adaptable to change as changes in the social systems require. A physical form that closely conforms to the processual aspects of the social system it would accommodate is likely to be a thing of beauty; for beauty is an inherent quality of a carefully conceived system.

3. *The third component of metropolitan spatial structure is the spatial configuration in which various types of activities are distributed.* When appropriately classified and weighted, a description of this component would record the places at which people do various kinds of things.[23] Stripped of the physical buildings and the land, both of which are typically subsumed in the term "land use," this is the "use" component.

It may be well to emphasize that I do mean to divorce "use" from "land" categorically. Land, as soil or as mineral resource, is closely related to "use" in agriculture or in mining. But for most urban activities "land" means only space and location on the surface of the earth.[24] To avoid the long-standing, and largely anachronistic, preoccupation with land, I prefer to regard it rigorously as soil and as topographic landscape only. In this more exact sense, it is, of course, an extremely powerful determinant in the total ecology.

The mode of activity classification would ideally seek to identify the economic functions performed, the social roles that participants are playing, and the levels of specialization of the participants.[25]

We have already noted that the configuration of activity locations within any given urban field is largely a function of the interaction patterns among the participants, since each establishment locates with an eye to maintaining efficient lines of communication with linked establishments. These communication lines, in turn, are mediated by the channels that are available. We have noted too that changes in activity locations are constrained by durability of the physical plant. But however integral the relationships of activity locations to other components of spatial structure, each component is analytically separable, and each is subject to systematic description over time.

A Descriptive Schema for Spatial Structure

This trichotomy of spatial structural components—describing the spatial patterns of (1) human interactions, (2) physical plant, and (3) activity locations—comprises the minimal framework for metropolitan spatial planning. Although somewhat more limited than Foley's broader conceptualization of spatial structure, together these three components furnish a useful, selective, and synoptic portrait as a basis for policy formulation and enunciation.

It is now necessary to search for the ways in which these might conceivably vary. I think there are only six hypothetically independent dimensions that are critical to each of the three components. In the list that follows, the horizontal rows use some rather arbitrary near-synonyms, as a way of avoiding confusion in discussion and as a way of assuring analytic consistency. By applying standardized measurement scales to each,[26] a metropolitan area's spatial structure could be systematically described (although not explained, of course) by reference to the degrees of variation along these twenty-four dimensions. Because the structural form of adapted spaces is different from that of physical channels, it is necessary to distinguish sharply between them and to construct separate measurements of each.

Dimensions of Spatial Structure

Process aspects	Form aspects		
	II. *Physical Component*		III. *Activity Component* (by type)
I. *Interaction Component* (by type)	A. Channels (by type)	B. Adapted Spaces (by type)	
a. Amplitude	a. Capacity	a. Capacity	a. Volume
b. Focality	b. Nucleation	b. Nucleation	b. Centralization
c. Subfocality	c. Subnucleation	c. Subnucleation	c. Subcentralization
d. Intensity	d. Concentration	d. Concentration	d. Density
e. Affinity	e. Clustering	e. Clustering	e. Localization
f. Insularity	f. Separation	f. Separation	f. Segregation

a. The quantities of each of the components are referred to in Ia, IIAa, IIBa, and IIIa; and these are probably self-explanatory. The most useful units for measurement are not apparent, however, for the unit must vary with the specific purpose of the analysis. Activities might be measured as numbers of people, dollar sales, value added, tons shipped, or in a number of other familiar ways. Standard measures of channel capacity are in use in the various industries, expressed as cubic feet, kilowatts, vehicles, railcars, messages, and so on, per hour. Interaction via persons- or goods-movement are readily expressed as numbers of people and tons of goods. Interaction via message transmission has no standardized unit of measure; but the "hubit" (human-hours times average "bits" of information received) seems promising.[27]

b. The second group refers to the degrees to which the components tend to pile up in major concentric forms.[28]

I.b. Focality of interaction relates to the degree to which messages, money flows, trips, or shipments cumulate around a single point in space. We might envision a map drawn by the cumulation of tracings made by each message, trip, or shipment as it moves through its channel from its origin to its destination.[29] The degree to which these tracings pile up around a single point then becomes the basis for measuring the degree of focality within the urban place.

Where a single major focus exists in a given settlement, the degree of focality of any specific type of flow is its propensity to cumulate around the point of greatest aggregate cumulation.

II.b. Nucleation of physical urban forms is universally recognized. In the aggregate, nucleation of adapted spaces refers to the degree to which all types of buildings and other urban spaces are agglomerated around a single point in space. At large scale, they comprise a visually observable collection of objects that can be seen from the air or from the highway on approaching an urban settlement. It is a grouping of buildings and other artifacts that differentiates the physical city from the countryside and industrial or residential districts from large open spaces. At finer scale, the multistoried buildings identify the nucleated physical form that marks the typical central business district of the large settlements.

In places where a physical nucleus exists, the degree of nucleation of any specific type of adapted space is the propensity of that type to occur at the center of the nucleus. Thus, for example, multistoried apartment buildings appear, on casual observation, to be less nucleated in Washington, D.C., and in Los Angeles than they are in Boston and Denver. In the former cities, the very tall apartment houses appear to be scattered quite widely throughout the physically urbanized area. In the latter cities, most of the very tall apartment houses appear to occur adjacent to the central business district.

Nucleation of channels is not always visually detectable, since so many of them are underground. Nonetheless, the spatial distribution of roads, railways, telephone lines, water lines, and so on, varies from high nucleation to low in different settlements; and variation in degree of nucleation among the several types within a given settlement is undoubtedly quite wide.

III.b. Centrality of urban activities relates to the degree to which activities tend to congregate around a single point in space. In the aggregate, an urban center is a congregation of activities around a single point. Centrality of any specific type of activity, then, is the propensity of that type of activity to locate at the point of maximum activity.

c. Subfocality, subnucleation, and subcentrality refer to the propensities of communications, physical artifacts, and activities to pile up at points of lesser concentration than the urban focus, the urban nucleus, and the urban center respectively. Similarly, the degree of subfocality, the degree of subnucleation, and the degree of subcentrality of any given types can be readily expressed with a number of standardized centrographic measurement scales.

It is important to note that I make no functional distinctions among these subaggregations according to the predominant activity conducted within them.[30] The only basis for classification within each component is simply size, which can vary along the continuum ranging from the very largest aggregation in New York to the smallest Navajo village in New Mexico. It is clear, of course, that functional differences are related to size; few skyscrapers are found in sub-subnuclei. But, as we shall see in Section IV, I find it necessary for my purposes here to make these distinctions independently.

d. Concentration and density are familiar concepts, referring, for example, to capacities of buildings or channels and to volumes of activities, respectively, per unit of space they occupy. *Intensity* is a somewhat different idea, referring to the amplitude of information generated by contacts between people at the occupied site with others at varying distances away. Concentration and density are thus *on-site* qualities. Intensity is a larger, spatial, yet *nonsite* quality, for it is a direct expression of the influence exerted by all communicators who are located at distant sites.

e. Degrees of affinity, clustering, and localization describe the relative *togetherness of like* interactions, channels or buildings, and activities, respectively. These are to be carefully distinguished from (*f.*) *insularity, separation, and segregation,* which describe the relative degrees of *mixture among unlike* types of interactions, channels or buildings, and activities.

These are hypothetically *independent* sets of dimensions. It is quite conceivable, for example, for a group of office buildings at a given high degree of clustering to be either mixed with store buildings or to be wholly separated from stores in an exclusive office conclave. Or they might be scattered at a constant low level of clustering, yet occur either intermixed with other building types or be separated from them. It should be clear, too, that the degree of clustering and the degree of separation are both hypothetically independent of the degree of concentration, just as localization, segregation, and density can hypothetically vary independently and as affinity, insularity, and intensity also can hypothetically vary independently.

The forms of our cities in the past have been relatively stable, and such changes as have occurred along any one of these dimensions have been accompanied by seemingly dependent changes along others. The refined descriptive analysis that I am calling for, however, may not have been as necessary in the past as it will be in the future. Patterns of functional interdependence will become increasingly complex at the same time that major developments in transportation and communication systems will be opening unprecedented possibilities for wholly new spatial patterns. If plans are to be made for new spatial structures in our large urban settlements compatible with the emerging new patterns of functional interdependence, we must explore the potentialities for change throughout the descriptive matrix, for the hypothetical independence of the dimensions may become empirical independence.

Much additional work needs to be done first to develop operational measurements for each of the twenty-four dimensions. Attempts must then be made to describe some existing metropolitan areas' spatial structures and then to expose changes that seem to be underway. Until such time as careful empirical measurements of these spatial dimensions are made, and until such time as the relation between formal and processual aspects of the various activities can be traced, metropolitan planning for spatial structure will continue to be severely handicapped by the crudity of the present language.

Our concern here has been with simple description of the complex phenomenon with which metropolitan planning is beginning to deal. We surely need a refined language with which we can depict the characteristics of the metropolitan place and through which we can express plans for it. The land-use-and-circulation-plan idiom is analytically far too coarse and it is incapable of dealing explicitly with the policy issues confronting metropolitan planners. If plans for the spatial aspects of a community are to get close to the heart of the community's economic and cultural life, they must present explicit policies for the spatial patterns of communications, as well as for the corresponding spatial arrangements of activity places and physical forms.

Throughout the discussion so far, I have dealt with the metropolitan area as an independently situated place. The descriptive schema I have presented is intended as a basis for improving our measurements and our understanding of the urban *settlement* and the urban *region,* as spatially limited *places.* But, however important this task is, I am nonetheless struck by the inadequacies of the place concepts of settlement and of region for dealing with the spatial patterns in which members of communities interact with each other and for undertaking functional analysis of urban places or regions. For, in a very important sense, the functional processes of urban communities are not placelike or regionlike at all.

III. URBAN REALMS: THE NONPLACE COMMUNITIES

The Interest-Communities

Both the idea of city and the idea of region have been traditionally tied to the idea of place. Whether conceived as physical objects, as interrelated systems of activities, as interacting populations, or as governmental dominions, a city or a region has been distinguishable from any other city or region by the fact of territorial separation.

The idea of community has similarly been tied to the idea of place. Although other conditions are associated with the community—including "sense of belonging," a body of shared values, a system of social organization, and interdependency

—spatial proximity continues to be considered a *necessary* condition.

But it is now becoming apparent that it is the accessibility rather than the propinquity aspect of "place" that is the necessary condition. As accessibility becomes further freed from propinquity, cohabitation of a territorial place—whether it be a neighborhood, a suburb, a metropolis, a region, or a nation—is becoming less important to the maintenance of social communities.

The free-standing town of colonial America may have fixed the images that are still with us.[31] At that time, when the difficulties and the costs of communicating and traveling were high, most of the townsman's associations were with other residents of the town he lived in. In turn, intratown intercourse tended to strengthen and stabilize the shared values and the systems of social organization; they must surely have reinforced the individual's "sense of belonging to his town." But even in colonial days when most men dealt solely with their neighbors, there were some who were simultaneously in close touch with others in distant towns, who were members of social communities that were not delimited to their home-town territories. As recently as two hundred years ago these long-distance communicators were uncommon, for the range of specialization and the range of interests among colonial populations were quite narrow. But today, the man who does not participate in such spatially extensive communities is the uncommon one.

Specialized professionals, particularly, now maintain webs of intimate contact with other professionals, wherever they may be. They share a particular body of values; their roles are defined by the organized structures of their groups; they undoubtedly have a sense of belonging to the groups; and, by the nature of the alliances, all share in a community of interests. Thus, these groups exhibit all the characteristics that we attribute to communities—except physical propinquity.

Spatial distribution is not the crucial determinant of membership in these professional societies, but interaction is. It is clearly no linguistic accident that "community" and "communication" share the Latin root *communis*, "in common." Communities comprise people with common interests who communicate with each other.

Though it is undoubtedly true that the most frequent interactions are among those members of professional communities who live and work within close distances of each other, the most productive contacts—those in which the content of the communication is the richest—are not necessarily the most frequent ones nor those that are made with associates who happen to be close by. Although specialized professionals are a rather extreme example, we can observe the same kinds of associational patterns among participants in the various types of nonprofessional communities as well.

All this is generally recognized. There is no novelty in noting that members of occupational groups are members thereby of limited-interest fraternities. Similarly, it is commonly recognized that members of churches, clubs, political parties, unions, and business organizations, and that hobbyists, sportsmen, and consumers of literature and of the performing arts are thereby also members of limited-interest groups whose spatial domains extend beyond any given urban settlement. A "true" community, on the other hand, is usually seen as a multi-interest group, somewhat heterogeneous, whose unity comes from interdependencies that arise among groups when they pursue their various special group interests *at a common place*.

I do not challenge the utility of this idea for certain purposes. A metropolis is indeed a complex system in which interrelated and interdependent groups support each other by producing and distributing a wide assortment of services, goods, information, friendships, and funds. Groups located in a given metropolis, where they carry out activities of all sorts, certainly do thereby create a systematic structure through which they work; they do indeed form a community whose common interests lie in continuing the operations of the place-based metropolitan system.

Nevertheless, the place-community represents only a limited and special case of the larger genus of communities, deriving its basis from the common interests that attach to propinquity alone. Those who live near each other share an interest in lowering the social costs of doing so, and they share an interest in the quality of certain services and goods that can be supplied only locally. It is this thread of common interests in traffic flow on streets, garbage collection, facilities for child rearing, protection from miscreant neighbors and from the inhospitable elements, and the like, that furnishes the reason-for-being of municipal government. This thread is also the basis for certain business firms and voluntary institutions that supply other goods and services which inhabitants and firms in the place-community demand with frequent recurrence. But, over time, these place-related interests represent a decreasing proportion of the total bundle of interests that each of the participants holds.

With few exceptions, the adult American is increasingly able to maintain selected contacts with others on an interest basis, over increasingly great distances; and he is thus a member of an increasing number of interest-communities that are not territorially defined. Although it is clear that some proportion of his time is devoted to associations with others in his place-community, several long-run changes seem to be underway that are cutting this proportion back. I need mention only rising educational levels and hence greater access to information and ideas; increasing amounts of non-working time; rising income levels that make long-distance communication and travel feasible, and the technological changes that are making them possible; and the weakening barriers to association across ethnic, racial, and class lines. These changes are expanding the range of diversity in the average person's associations and are inducing a parallel reduction in the relative importance of place-related interests and associations.

Although each generation of Americans participates in more substantively and spatially diverse communities than did its predecessor, there is at any point in time a wide range of variation among contemporaries. Today there are people whose lives and interests are only slightly more diverse than those of their eighteenth-century counterparts; there are the notorious Brooklynites who, except for contacts through television, movies, and the other mass media, have never crossed the East River.[32] But there are others who are at home throughout the world.

I suspect that the spatial range of intercourse varies directly as some function of a person's level of specialization—that the more highly skilled a person is or the more uncommon the information he holds, the more spatially dispersed are his interest-communities and the greater are the distances over which he interacts with others. This is because specialization is equivalent to rarity, and the customers for the rare service or the participants in a rare activity that requires highly specialized knowledge are likely to be territorially far-flung.

Thus there seems to be a hierarchical continuum in which the most highly specialized people are participants in interest-communities that span the entire world; others, who are somewhat less specialized, seldom communicate with people outside the nation but interact regularly with men in various parts of the country; others seldom directly communicate with anyone outside the metropolitan settlement; and still others communicate almost exclusively with their neighbors. Compare the people engaged in virus research, pharmaceutical production, wholesale drug distribution, and retail drug distribution. The participants in all these activities might work in the same town or indeed in the same neighborhood within the same town. But the spaces over which their important interactions take place extend from the world to the neighborhood, depending upon the specialization level of the information being communicated or the goods being marketed.

In his role as a member of a world-wide community of virus researchers, the scientist is not a member of his place-community at all. The fact that his laboratory is located in a given town or metropolis may be almost irrelevant to maintaining the crucial linkages with men in other places who are also probing the frontiers of knowledge in his field.[33] He may also be in close contact with colleagues in his laboratory who are also active participants in the world-wide community and who comprise a subgroup within that larger community. Of course, he and they also rely upon a large number of assistants, suppliers, and service people of various types, some of whom also work in the place-community. But the contacts with these people operate at lesser levels of specialization, and thus the scientists and they, in turn, are simultaneously members of other interest-communities.

Our virus researcher is a member of a great many such communities, each of which may function at a different level of specialization and over differing distances. As contributor to and reader of his professional literature, he is a member of the world-community of virus researchers. He may travel a great deal to diverse points on the globe to advise governments or firms, to talk with colleagues, or to participate in conferences. It is likely, too, that he participates in a variety of other world-communities in the arts, in literature, in foreign relations, and so on. He also participates in his national professional affairs, advises governments and firms in America, participates in the art, literary, and political activities of the nation, and thus interacts within a large number of interest-communities whose members communicate over the space that is roughly encompassed by the United States territory. In turn he is a member of many additional less specialized communities; as a member of his local PTA, he is a participant in the place-related community of the town where he resides.[34]

Depending, then, upon the *role* that he is playing, our biochemist friend is a member of one or another of a great many different communities, each of which functions through a different range of spatial distances. For that portion of his *time* devoted to place-community roles, he is a member of that place-community. For the portions of his time in which he plays roles in other communities, he is *not* a member of his place-community.

The Urban Realms

At any given level of specialization there is a wide variety of interest-communities whose members conduct their affairs within roughly the same spatial field. They share common market or service areas; in some degree they are interdependent and interact with each other; and, at their respective levels of specialization, each heterogeneous group of interest-communities makes up a complex, but organized, system of activities and intercourse. I shall refer to these communities of interest-communities as *urban realms*.

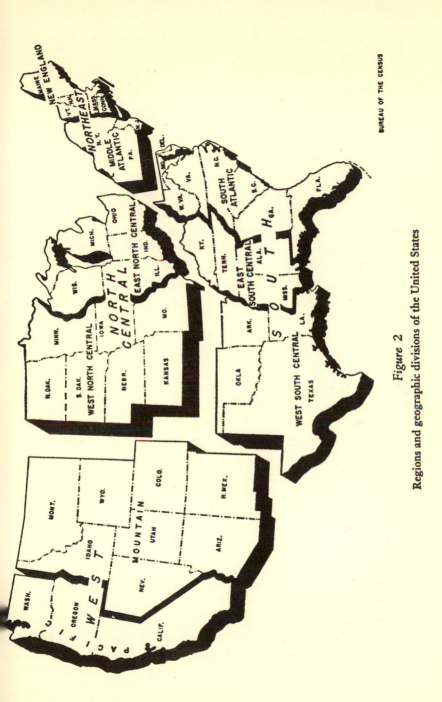

Figure 2

Regions and geographic divisions of the United States

It is apparent that the urban realms are analogous to the urban regions, being somewhat similar in function but dissimilar in structure. Both refer to functionally interdependent activities and actors operating in spatial fields, but the compositions of activities and actors and the extents of the spatial fields are very different.

An urban region, comprising an urban settlement and its surrounding hinterland, is a spatially delimited territory. Although the margins are always indistinct and overlap, at any given level in the hierarchy of urban regions each urban region is territorially discrete; except at their margins, no two urban regions encompass the same territory. The Census Bureau's map, showing its national regional divisions, dramatically expresses the pure idea of territorial assignment (see Figure 2). To my knowledge, no similar map has been prepared for the urban regions in the United States, but such a map would similarly divide the total territory into segments, each land area being assigned to its appropriate urban node in the manner of Christaller's formulation (Figure 3). In all these, every person inhabiting a given place is assigned to that place exclusively, irrespective of his level of specialization. The urban region thus reflects a unitary idea. A given urban place with its surrounding hinterland may nest within a larger hierarchy of places and hinterlands, but it is nonetheless a unitary place in a strict Euclidean sense. At any instant in time, its spatial extent is essentially fixed, and its composition can be determined by a census of the population and establishments located there.

An urban realm, in contrast, is neither urban settlement nor territory, but heterogeneous groups of people communicating with each other through space. At any of the lower levels in the hierarchical continuum of specialization, the spatial distances over which the people interact are relatively short; but the spatial extent of each realm is ambiguous, shifting instantaneously as participants in the realm's many interest-communities make new contacts, trade with different customers, socialize with different friends, or read different publications.

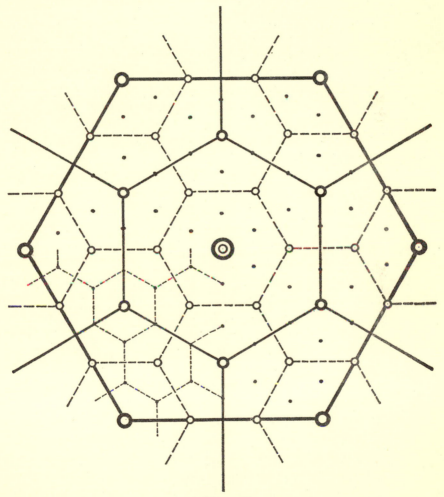

Figure 3
Hexagonal schema of Christaller's system of central places

Similarly, the population composition of the realm is never stable from one instant in time to the next. Every person is at different moments a communicant in any of several different realms, *as he shifts from one role to another*. This is, of course, especially true of the highly specialized man who may turn from a transatlantic telephone call to arbitrate an intra-office personnel problem, then read his mail from customers in various places, then join the other motorists in the peak-hour traffic rush, before reassuming his roles as parent, newspaper reader, and member of a friendship circle. The participants in each realm are constantly shifting; but not everyone participates in the world-realm, although the neighborhood-realms include virtually all persons during some part of their days. Moreover, there are very few who devote a large proportion of their time to world-realm roles, but there are very large numbers of people who devote large proportions of their time to roles associated with local realms.

It should now be apparent that most large urban settlements include residents who communicate with others throughout the entire hierarchical array of realms. In some degree, then, probably best conceived as the proportion of man-hours devoted to playing out roles associated with the affairs of each realm, each settlement is the partial locus of realms at many levels in the hierarchy. In this context, then, no urban settlement is a unitary place. Rather, it is a part of a whole array of shifting and interpenetrating realm-spaces.

Figure 4 is a representation of the idea I am trying to communicate. Contrary to the *vertical* divisions of territory that accord with place conceptions of region (as in Figure 2), I view the functional processes within the total national urban space as *horizontally* stratified. Thus, the most specialized people communicate across the entire nation and beyond. At lesser levels of specialization, people interact over shorter

Figure 4

Geographic space extends horizontally and level of specialization vertically in the drawing. The bars then represent the realms which extend in overlapping patterns across the continent, those at the highest levels being spatially most extensive. Individuals participate in first one then another realm, as they play first one role, then another. The spatial patterns of realms are thus indistinct and unstable.

distances, but the extent varies from person to person and, for any given person, from moment to moment. We thus find no Euclidean territorial divisions—only continuous variation, spatial discontinuity, persisting disparity, complex pluralism, and dynamic ambiguity.

Seen in a communications context then, the urban settlement is far from being a unitary place. Its composition and its spatial dimensions are relative to the observations of participants in different realms at different instants in time.

Directions for Empirical Observation

I would like to be able to estimate the proportions of man-hours at various locations that are devoted to roles associated with realms at the various levels. It will be an extremely difficult task to do so empirically; elaborate survey research methods would be necessary to identify self-images of roles and to estimate time allocations. But at this stage in our deliberations the operational difficulties are not of pressing concern. The reader may find it helpful to think, instead, of a special kind of real income that can substitute as a rough approximation.

In a very gross way, dollar income varies directly with level of skill and with rarity of the information a person holds; but money income is far from precise, and it is not the only contributor to income. To account for the imprecision in dollar incomes among such people as low-paid but highly specialized college professors and well-paid but relatively unspecialized salesmen, we should have to add the dollar equivalents of the other income that each receives, such as the professor's work satisfaction, freedom from restraint, flexible schedule, and the various amenities he enjoys. In addition, income received in the form of information—the cultural wealth that we discussed earlier—would undoubtedly bulk

large in any kind of comparative accounting. The professor
receives a great deal of his income through words rather
than through dollars; and even though his salary check may
be far smaller than the used-car salesman's, he is, in this sense,
far the wealthier man.

Adequate data on money income are only now beginning
to be made available, and they are still quite insufficient. Data
on information-income are not available at all, but R. L. Meier
has offered some imaginative suggestions for constructing estimates for population aggregates that are conceptually applicable to individuals as well.[35]

For the purpose of constructing order-of-magnitude estimates of the volumes of information received through the
public communication channels, he proposes that messages
flowing through those channels be systematically sampled and
subjected to analysis that would measure their information
content. The standard unit of information, the "bit," furnishes
the basis for estimating the gross volume of content; the
typical number of bits in each class of publicly transmitted
message is potentially knowable.[36] So, too, is the average number of man-hours devoted to receiving each class of message.
Numbers of bits received per hour times number of human-
hours devoted to their reception might be made to yield a
new unit of social accounting, the "hubit," which, in turn,
is potentially a basis for computing the cultural value of the
information receipts.[37]

Although our capacities for constructing such a measurement are rapidly increasing, systematic estimates of these sorts
have not yet been made. Furthermore, it may never be possible to convert dollar, information, and other incomes to a
standard unit; and anyway, for the present at least, none of
these data bases for estimating total real income is adequate.

So, in an effort to clarify these concepts, let us temporarily side-step the empirical difficulties and simply assume some miraculous statistical invention that would permit us to place the nation's total mixture of human-role-hours through something akin to the petroleum engineer's fractionating column. If we could distill out those at the very top of the specialization hierarchy (those that are the most volatile?), we could then identify the time fraction of those people having the rarest skills and the rarest information who play out roles associated with the highest realms. It is these people, as we have noted before, who devote some proportion of their time to sending messages to others throughout the world and who are therefore the most spatially rarefied. In addition to high officials in the State Department and in the large corporations, our distillate would surely include our virus researcher; for, at the moment of discovery, when he is the only person in the world who holds a specific bit of knowledge, he is a very rare man indeed.

Then, if we were to distill off the next fraction, we could in turn identify the time fraction of those people whose most rarefied realm is the nation. This second distillate would be larger than the first, including most of the first plus the millions of other men who play roles that bring them into contact with others throughout the country. By continuing to boil our population mixture we would separate out the time fractions of men at lesser and lesser levels of specialization until we distill off the people who never interact with others outside their neighborhood realms.[38]

For convenience only, we conduct our distillation process as though there were a discrete set of realms, but here, as with petroleum, the mixture is so fine-grained that the levels comprise a continuum rather than a series of fractional classes.

There is indeed a hierarchy of realms, but they are not likely to exhibit a step structure; when plotted, the series would resemble a children's slide rather than a staircase. If we were to array the total distribution of man-hours devoted to participation in realms at the various levels, we would probably find a frequency pattern somewhat like that shown in Figure 5.

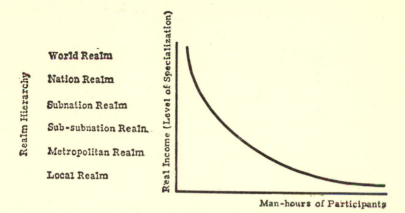

Figure 5

The hierarchical continuum of realms

Three additional refinements are now called for. (1) Having distilled out the communicators in each realm level, let us press our analogy to petroleum processing still further and subject these people to qualitative analysis in an effort to identify the interest-community composition of the mixture of people. (2) When we have done that, let us then identify the places at which each participant is located. (3) And then, in an effort to evaluate the richness of the various parts of the spatial field, let us apply an appropriate set of weights to the spatial distribution.

1) The qualitative analysis would separate all the people who, as members of an interest-community, interact with others on the basis of that common substantive interest. Thus the analysis would reveal all participants in an industry—whether finance, metallurgy, electronics, or used cars—and all participants sharing other interests—whether stamp collecting, music, baseball, or foreign affairs. The mode and the degree of refinement of the classification of interests would depend upon the purposes of the analysis and on our analytic skills. The effect of this qualitative analysis would be to stratify the exponential distribution vertically, in this fashion (Figure 6).

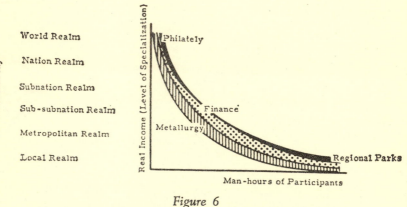

Figure 6

The interest-community composition of realms

One of the interest-communities may then be extracted and considered separately (Figure 7).

Even though the realms form a continuum, for simplicity of graphic exposition, let us make some arbitrary divisions, apply them to this interest-community, and simultaneously expand the scale on the X-axis (Figure 8).

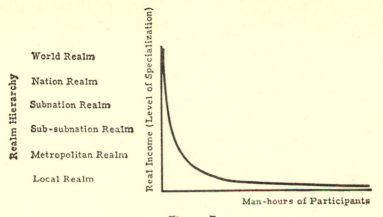

Figure 7

An interest-community, by realm

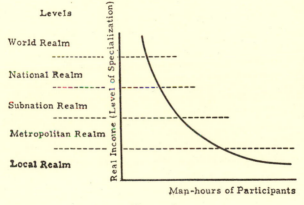

Figure 8

An interest-community, by arbitrary realm divisions

This figure can then be converted into a bar graph showing the number of man-hours devoted to activities of the interest-community within the United States (Figure 9).

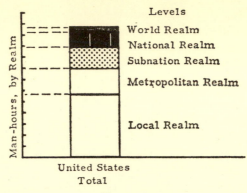

Figure 9

An interest-community, by arbitrary realm divisions

2) We can now draw upon our hypothetical data on places at which participants operate and distribute the total United States man-hours to their approximately mapped locations (Figure 10).

Certain contributors to the gross locational patterns shown in this map profile are of course already known from census-type sources that report man-hours expended as paid employment. But this map is quite different from an ordinary activity-location map. In addition to recording the locations of members of interest-communities who are producers of goods, services, or information, it simultaneously shows the locations of those members who are their consumers. As a reflection of communication among participants, it is a simultaneous portrait of both senders' and receivers' locations. This is apparent if we consider the communities associated with such interests as stamp collecting, music, literature, sports, current events, professional affairs, and others in which the production-consumption dichotomy is less institutionalized. But it is equally true in steel, petroleum, and finance. Hence the map records locations of participants throughout the national territory for many activities whose production facilities may be highly localized, and the portrait is therefore considerably different from the typical activity-location map.[39]

The locational pattern of interactions associated with the conduct of any given activity at any given place is seldom a simple yes-no phenomenon, that is, the question is not *whether* an interest-community is represented at a given place. More likely, the proper questions are *how much* participation occurs at all locations and how spatially extensive is the intercourse among the participants.

To illustrate further, let us consider an activity system and try to anticipate the locational patterns of interaction associated with it. Since the securities market is probably among the most highly centered and localized of any, it offers a good example; for, despite its centering and localization, its linkages interlace the continent. Dealers at the major stock exchanges in New York are in virtually perpetual contact with men in smaller exchanges in a few major cities and with brokerage offices throughout the nation. But because the nature of the business requires close watch on all aspects of the economy, and indeed on all events that might lead others to believe that others might believe that an event might influence the economy or a firm, the web of communications that employees in the financial world maintain is virtually ubiquitous. Simultaneously, of course, every business firm and every stockholder is in touch with the financial establishments on his own, and their spatial distribution is also virtually ubiquitous. Thus, despite the clear fact that the major establishments engaged in securities exchange are very highly centered and

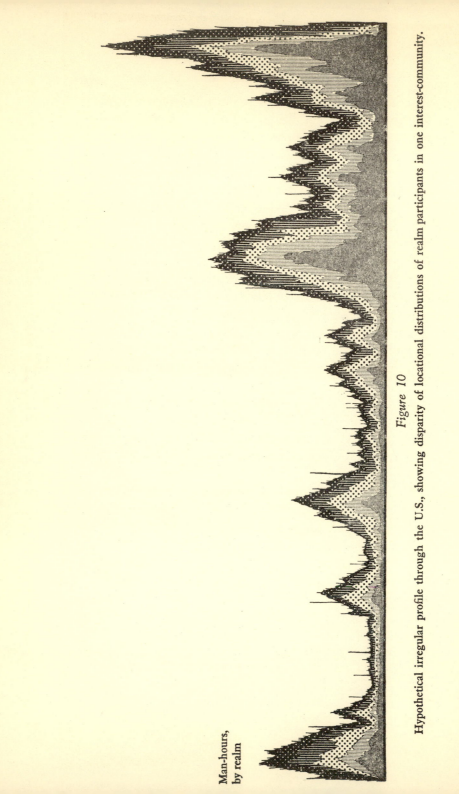

Man-hours, by realm

Figure 10

Hypothetical irregular profile through the U.S., showing disparity of locational distributions of realm participants in one interest-community.

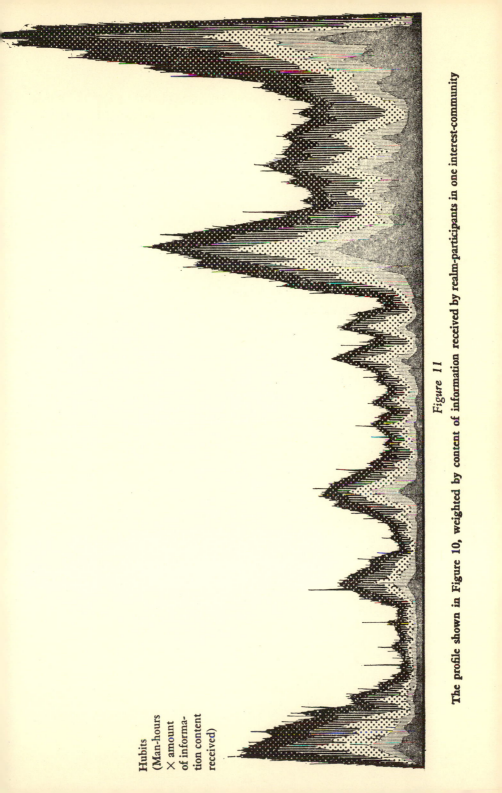

Hubits
(Man-hours
× amount
of informa-
tion content
received)

Figure 11

The profile shown in Figure 10, weighted by content of information received by realm-participants in one interest-community localized, and that the spatial patterns of linkages to the stock exchanges exhibit high focality and high affinity, there is still an important nonfocal pattern that prevails.

If the securities exchanges be thought to be a special case, consider the network of communications involved in the processes of education, biological research, steel production, entertainment, business management, federal government, or any of the other interest-communities within the national realm.

3) Having located the participants in the various interest-communities by realm levels, we must now apply some appropriate weights in an effort to determine the intensity of their participation. Since I have defined realm participation to be a function of real income and since I have accounted for absolute-content of information-received as a component of real income, an information weighting is already built into the schema. But no assignment of information content has been specifically made to an individual's interest-community or his participation in any particular realm, and none has been specifically made to his participation at any given place. Again, Meier's "hubit" is suggestive, being related to the relative cultural richness of messages received.

It is helpful to imagine a map, of the sort shown in profile in Figure 10, as being specifically weighted for the average number of bits of information received or sent per hour, in association with the activities of each interest-community at each realm level. If we were to imagine the map profile in Figure 10 being so weighted by information content, it would undergo considerable revision, as suggested in Figure 11. Here, within a single interest-community, man-hours devoted to participation at the world realm would be weighted considerably more heavily than those at the local realm. If the interest-community were finance, the local-realm participants would include the janitors, elevator operators, file clerks, tellers, and other relatively unspecialized employees of banks. World-realm participants would include bank executives who negotiate with corporation executives in distant places, and the content of their messages is considerably richer and more value-filled. Or, if this example should seem inadequate, consider again the virus researcher and the bottle washer in his laboratory.

Such weighting for information content would permit us to compare the relative intensity levels of human interaction at various places and to assess the relative levels of focality among places. The degrees of focality are probably highly variable among places and among the interest-communities at any given place. For example, despite its ubiquitous feelers, the securities-exchange activities are highly focal at New York, and the gradient declines very rapidly. Higher education is multifocal, there being several major subfocal peaks in the Boston to Philadelphia area, and the gradient is considerably less sharp.

A map showing the spatial distribution of information-weighted man-hours devoted to participation in the various interest-communities at the various realm levels would be a valuable resource indeed. It would permit comparative measurements, among urban *places,* for each of the six interaction dimensions shown in Table 1. These in turn might be compared with comparable measurements of the other three components of spatial structure, and the relations among these components might then be explored.

Comparative measurements of this sort are potentially valuable contributors to improved understanding of the relations between the functional processes of urban societies and the locational-physical forms of the settlements. And if such studies should reveal, as I strongly suspect they would, that rich and diverse human interaction can be experienced under conditions of low density and low concentration and even low centrality or subcentrality, we might be led to prepare quite different plans for our metropolitan settlements. If we regard "urbanity" as a characteristic of urban life rather than of urban form, and if we define "urbanity" more specifically as a function of the diversity and the volume of information that an individual receives, we might discover that Los Angelenos enjoy as urbane a life as do New Yorkers. Our evaluations of the Los Angeles settlement's spatial form would surely then have to be considerably revised.

IV. THE RELEVANCE TO METROPOLITAN PLANNING

Concerning Territory, Place, Boundaries, and Governments

Charged with recommending policies to guide governmental action, planners have been searching for useful concepts that might order their thinking. As I have noted before, the most generally accepted conceptions of the urban phenomenon are closely tied to the more fundamental ideas of land and territory; of unitarily discrete and nodally concentric place; and of a Euclidean-Newtonian system of order that relies upon bounded categories and whose dimensions remain stable.

The idea that each territorially nodal settlement should be governed by a single, separate municipality is a clear expression of these concepts; the proposal that each metropolitan settlement should similarly be governed by a separate unit is largely a territorial expansion of the same idea. The fundamental concepts are reflected, too, in the typical general plan that recommends a segregated land-use pattern; but the fascination with the proposals for new towns amidst a green-belt and for unitary neighborhoods delineated by sharply bounded parks and highways is probably the most dramatic expression.

So rigidly implanted are these fundamental concepts, even among the urban social scientists who have sought understanding of functional interdependencies, that many will regard notions of a nonplace community and of a spatially discontinuous city as internally contradictory, nonsense propositions. And yet, in some contexts, we have become quite accustomed to these ideas. The structures and functions of governments will serve to illustrate this fact.

Governmental jurisdictions have traditionally been territorially based and bounded. The origins of the tradition probably lie in the need for protection against marauding strangers; in the desires of peoples who depend upon farming, mining, or forestry to maintain exclusive use of the soils and waters that their livelihoods depend upon; and in the protectionist aim of peoples who share certain value systems to exclude peoples having different value systems. There undoubtedly are other origins, but these have certainly been among the important ones.

In a day when cultures within the United States were markedly different and when most people were engaged in extractive industries, local land-based governments were more predominant than they are today. The interests of inhabitants within a town were quite different from those of nearby farmers. Similarly, the interests of inhabitants in different towns might have been considerably different. But as the range of cultural differences among urbanites has narrowed, the needs for protection have lessened. As the life styles of farmers have become more like those of city dwellers, the cultural distinctions that once differentiated the urban from the rural are fading.

We have previously observed that, increasingly, interests and associations are being formed on other than locational bases and, in the corollary observation, that locational places are the sites of many communities having increasingly disparate interests. *All* residents of a place hold common interests only in the conditions of that place, and it is these conditions that municipalities seek to regulate and guide. State governments represent the interests of larger place-communities, but again their jurisdictions are largely limited to the place-related conditions; in turn national government represents the place-related interests of the inhabitants of the nation. This concern for the interests of hierarchical place-communities is one of the important motivations that underlay the original federalist idea. But an important governmental overlay has been developing, although not always in the cloak of government.

Henrik Blum stated this well when he observed that "each problem defines its own community for solution," and he might have added, each group of interests defines its own community for satisfaction. We have seen the rise of corporations, clubs, churches, trade associations, unions, and a large variety of less formal organizations, created on an interest basis and without limitations of territorial jurisdictions. All these are governments of special sorts. The system of elementary and secondary education operated by the Catholic Church is a dramatic instance, because it happens to parallel a function performed by local public-school boards; but, unlike the school board, it does so without territorial restraint. A trade association that regulates an industry is parallel to a state or federal regulatory commission, although it represents a different group of publics. The list of such nonterritorial governments is almost endless.

Not all of them are outside public governments, of course, for a major expansion of jurisdictions has been underway, especially in the federal government. As the public body encompassing the largest territory, it thereby also encompasses the realm spaces through which many interest-communities interact. It has thus, at least within the boundaries of the United States, been able to operate as a nonplace government. It constructs major public works, wherever they may be needed; it undertakes public health programs wherever disease needs curbing; it controls certain industries' operations without regard for the locations of the industries' plants; it participates in urban renewal and housing developments, wherever the demands occur; it sets standards for welfare services wherever the services are offered. And where international concerns arise, we have recently seen the United Nations conduct a variety of public-welfare programs with scarce regard for national boundaries; the European Common Market is clearly another such effort selectively to break the barriers of unitary, land-based governmental boundaries.

At approximately the realm level of the metropolitan interest-communities, we are now seeing a rising interest in a new government that would encompass the large land-based settlement. The interest in metropolitan government is largely a response to the limitations inherent in small place-bounded governments and an effort to create an action body capable of dealing systematically with problems of the larger settlement place. Thus it is frequently suggested that a metropolitan government should remain aloof from the problems of neighborhood place-communities, leaving jurisdiction over matters of refuse collection, local streets, small parks, fire fighting, and the like, to local municipalities. Instead, the metropolitan government would selectively limit its jurisdiction to constructing those public works and conducting those welfare programs in which all or most members of the larger place-community have a common interest. In addition, just about everybody's list of appropriate activities for such a larger-place government includes metropolitan spatial planning.[40]

Metropolitan government would thus be added to an already vast array of existing governments. Some of the governments are territorially bounded, others are free to serve all potential markets within the national territory; some limit their activities to the concerns of specific interest-communities, others perform a large array of services; some are constitutionally public, others are private, and still others are neither public nor private but some mixture of both.[41] Within this unarticulated array of governments, metropolitan government is seen as an articulated, territorially and functionally bounded authority. Its territorial basis derives from the concept of a hierarchy of nested regions. Its functional basis derives from the concept of the metropolitan place-community.

It is not seen as a government for the metropolitan realm, however, for its jurisdictions would be limited to but one of the interest-communities that comprise the metropolitan realm —that community of interest which surrounds the settlement place. Moreover, the realm extends far beyond the major settlement, and the metropolitan government's boundaries would not.

As an activity of metropolitan government, metropolitan planning would be similarly delimited in territory and in substantive concern. It is typically conceived as a territorially enlarged version of city planning, but devoted instead to those place-related interests that are shared by all the residents in all parts of the metropolitan settlement.

It is thus very likely that early metropolitan planning activities will be restricted to formulating plans and programs for the locations of activities and of certain physical facilities. But, as I have sought to demonstrate in Section II above, effective planning for locational-physical form would properly begin with planning for the spatial processes of interaction. And it should now be apparent, from the discussion in Section III, that the spatial patterns of interaction can best be understood by examining the realm-participation of the various populations within the metropolitan place.

I thus see metropolitan planning, during the next decade, as a governmental activity focused on the metropolitan place, yet seeking to accommodate place-conditions to the nonplace interactions of the inhabitants. Let me elaborate on this relationship and point to some inherent problems by examining some questions surrounding the planned locations of urban centers within a metropolitan regional place.

The Classification of Centers

Any metropolitan planning activity must deal with the patterns of centering, subcentering, and noncentering as the form expressions of some major current policy issues. There are other key decision areas, to be sure, but the centering dimension of spatial structure will serve to illustrate the point.

It is by no means clear what was meant by an "urban center" in the past. Central-place theorists have always been quick to identify the central activity cluster within each physically identifiable urban node. But centers that become absorbed into large, physically contiguous settlement patterns somehow soon lose their identity, or at least they seem to lose their interest for students of urban structure. Clearly, it matters not whether the residential settlement surrounding a business district happens to be in turn surrounded by a greenbelt of farms or by more houses that adjoin another business district. The nature of the first district is not necessarily affected by its immediate neighbors. Oddly, if the district is the major activity cluster in an incorporated municipality, it tends to retain its identity in urban analysis more successfully than if it is absorbed within the territory encompassed by a larger municipality. But no matter. For our purposes it should be clear that the vicinity of an urban center or its governmental status directly reveals little about its functions —about what goes on there.

I have defined a center as the aggregation of activities around some point in space, and subcenters as smaller aggregations around other points in space. For some purposes this may be sufficient, but a description of centering patterns in these terms would reveal little about the linkages among the establishments located in these places.

Less commonly, and more fruitfully, the attempt has been made to distinguish among types of urban centers in accordance with the number of different types of activities that are located in each. Hence, within a large urban settlement we can easily identify the major concentration of activities as also being the most various, and a hierarchical set of centers can be identified ranging down from it to the neighborhood shopping center.

Certain specialized activities tend to be found most commonly in the higher-order centers; more standardized activities tend to be found in the lower-order ones. The stock exchanges, for example, are typically located in the largest, most specialized centers; grocery stores and appliances outlets are found in the more numerous centers where standardized goods and services are offered. There has therefore been an effort to classify centers according to the types of economic functions that are performed in each. But real analytic difficulties arise, since a classification by industry type does not distinguish degrees of specialization within the industry. Finance, for example, is not the exclusive function of high-order centers, as we have noted before and as the banking system of California demonstrates with its thousand-odd branch banks distributed among the local shopping centers. The same classification problem arises within almost every other industry group, professional services of all types included.

The more sophisticated approaches have therefore sought to distinguish each center's place in the hierarchy of centers according to the territorial market extent of the establishments that are located there. This was Christaller's model,[42] and it was McKenzie's[43] and Bogue's.[44] In any given center, the larger the number of establishments having an extensive market area, the higher is the center's position within the hierarchy of centers. This conception recognizes the variations in specialization among participants within each industry, or activity, group. It approaches the analysis of urban centers by examining the patterns of interaction between occupants of the center and those outside. But its limitation derives from its having been restricted to the examination of the center-hinterland relationships, that is, to a classification of the hierarchy of center places.

With quite inadequate data, to be sure, my colleagues and I thus classified the existing centers in the San Francisco Bay Area at the time the Bay Area Regional Plan was being prepared for the 1955 Transit Study. We subsequently prepared a plan proposing an expanded hierarchy of such center places.[45] It was relatively easy to classify the central district of San Francisco as the "regional center," to classify central Oakland as a "subregional center," and in turn to classify a large number of other central districts at a third-order level; we called them "district centers." But it was difficult to understand what this catalogue of centers really meant. We knew full well that not all the people who interact with others throughout the region are located at San Francisco and that not all activities located there are region serving, but we did not know then how to get around the ambiguity that the title "regional center" carried. It is quite true that a great many of the highly specialized establishments are indeed located at San Francisco, but a very great many that are even more specialized are located in many other places throughout the region: in Berkeley, on the Peninsula, in San Jose, even in Milpitas.

Many of the specialists located in the Bay Area do not participate in the metropolitan realm at all, their linkages being primarily with Washington or New York or Hong Kong or with their local-residence realms. Some of these specialists are located in the Bay Area because of the amenities that the place affords and because they rely upon submetropolitan realms for a complex assortment of services that are available there. These participants in the world realm and the nation realm happen to be placed within the Bay Area, but their primary community is outside. In this sense, to the degree that they function as participants in these highly rarefied realms and interact with others who are spatially removed from their activity places, they are not at all a part of the Bay Area place-community, or even of the so-called Bay Area hinterland—contrary to the Christaller and McKenzie conceptions.

For purposes of comparison, Figure 12 restates Christaller's hexagonal distribution; and, within the same geometric pat-

```
   BCD     D      D     BCD
     D    D    CD     D     D
  D    CD    D     D    CD     D
BCD   D      D   ABCD    D      D   BCD
   D    CD     D     D    CD     D
     D     D    CD     D     D
     BCD     D     D    BCD
```

I.

Christaller's hierarchical system of central places.

Each letter represents an economic function, having a market-extent of relatively consistent territorial scale.

```
      WZ    WZ    XZ   WXYZ
   WYZ  XYZ    Z    XYZ    XZ
  Z    XZ   WXZ  WXYZ  WXYZ  WXYZ
XYZ    YZ  WXYZ WXYZ WXYZ  WYZ  WXZ
  WYZ WXYZ XYZ    Z    WXZ  WXYZ
    WZ   WYZ   WYZ  WXYZ   YZ
    WXZ    XZ   WYZ   WYZ
```

II.

Hypothesized distribution of realm-participants.

Each letter represents a degree of specialization of the participants in *all* types of activities (interest-communities). The geometrically hexagonal pattern is followed only for direct comparison with the Christaller distribution.

If the scale across the diagram were 25 miles, the territory might be one that is typically classified as a metropolitan area. The symbols represent participants in realms at various levels of specialization, arbitrarily grouped into classes: "W," world realm; "X," nation realm; "Y," metropolitan realm; and "Z," local place realm.

Figure 12

Two hypothetical patterns of activity distribution

tern, it portrays the activity-place pattern that I hypothesize to exist in a typical metropolitan area. The diagram suggests the locational disparity of participants in the various realms, whether in places like San Francisco, Oakland, Stockton, or Berkeley. The numbers of high-order specialists in these places would of course vary considerably, and the relative intensities of human interactions associated with the realm-related activities would also vary widely. But, viewed in their *locational* patterns, these activities are certainly more widely dispersed in the United States today than Christaller's scheme would suggest. With respect to the local-realm participation, however, the Christaller distribution and mine are the same.

This being so, it seems inaccurate to assign their activity-related interactions to the individual centers within the Bay Area at which they are located. More precisely, selected persons, for some proportion of their time, are a part of higher-order realms, and the entire Bay Area region is therefore subfocus within the world and nation realms.

But what of those whose market area is more local in extent? Even here, a unitary classification seems untenable. Participants in the metropolitan realm are not located exclusively in San Francisco; they too are distributed throughout the urbanized area and beyond. They deal with customers and clients and colleagues and cousins wherever they may be, irrespective (by definition, or by distillation) of where within the region they are located. It is quite true that many, and perhaps most, are located in the highly accessible San Francisco central district, but not all of them are. We can be confident, however, that were we to trace the interaction patterns, as opposed to mapping their place locations, their information flows would peak to a focal point at central San Francisco. But the field of interaction would cover the entire realm, and smaller foci would show up at a great many points throughout the field.

Seen as an interaction system, then, rather than as a locational pattern of activity places, the attempt to delineate the regional center and its hinterland is transposed to an attempt to delineate the *focal pattern* of realm participants over the space field. Rather than a center-place, we portray the degree of focality of interactions throughout the realm's space. We thereby remove the unitary restrictions imposed by having to assign regional primacy or dominance to one place within the region, in the face of the dispersed locational pattern of realm participants. By treating the patterns of concentricity as *field* phenomena, rather than as point, or place, phenomena, we are able to free ourselves from the strictures of the old conceptual systems that were based upon the fundamentalist concepts of land, place, and boundary.

The effect of this type of analysis, it should be clear, is to discard the notion of hinterland for purposes of interaction analysis. The hinterland has been, by definition, a place demarcated by interaction with a center. This may have been a more valid conception at the time when urban settlements were small, when their inhabitants were less specialized than they are today, and when all specialized persons lived in the nodal settlement and served the surrounding farmers. But today, when highly specialized communicators are to be found in what is called hinterland, the basis for the definition dissipates. Increasingly in the future, when high-level specialists are able to locate their establishments in outlying settlements or even in the mountains, as at least one electronics research group already has in the Sierra, what is hinterland and what is center becomes, at best, but a difference in magnitudes of information flow and of volumes of activity. For, *in kind*, the world-realm participants and the metropolitan-realm participants in the mountains and those in the large central business district are the same.

Depicted in a realm map, in which contour lines reflect

intensities of interaction patterns traversing a space field, the form of the urban realm would clearly be something other than the classical center-plus-hinterland. In most contemporary metropolitan realms the form of the contour map's surface would be highly irregular, reflecting focal, subfocal, and non-focal patterns that extend throughout the geographic space of the realm. In the San Francisco Bay Area, the spatial interaction patterns of *metropolitan-realm* participants extend to include Stockton, Reno, and the High Country. Seen in this light, then, none of northern California can be called San Francisco's hinterland. Rather, all of northern California is integral with the entire metropolitan realm. And this would include those interactions that emanate from Berkeley and Palo Alto as well as those radiating out of San Francisco and Stockton.

Similar surfaces would undoubtedly be found for the lower-level realms whose spatial extents do not reach much beyond the physically urbanized territory surrounding San Francisco Bay. Instead of a tidy, nested hierarchy of submetropolitan places, each with its focus, center, and nucleus, we would find spatially disparate patterns, made the more equivocal because the spatial extents of the various interest-communities fail to coincide and fail to remain stable through time. If we could construct measurements of the spatial patterns of information flow associated with these local realms, we would undoubtedly find focal, multifocal, and nonfocal patterns; and we would find considerable variation in levels of intensity, of affinity, and of insularity.

In this way, the puzzle that concerned us in the Bay Area regional plan studies may be at least partially solved. Where we might fail to classify activity centers within a tidy functional hierarchy, we can view the interaction component of spatial structure as reflecting the spatial patterns of realm-specific interactions within such a functional hierarchy. Rather than describe metropolitan spatial structure solely within the limitations of place conceptions, as we must in treating activity and physical locational patterns in settlements and in regions, we can supplement our analyses by viewing the distribution of human activities as spatially structured processes of human interaction.

Such an approach, I believe, can bring us closer to the crucial welfare issues of urban life that metropolitan planning must deal with. It can give us a more comprehensive, descriptive base from which to plan for the spatial structure of metropolitan communities. And, perhaps most important of all, a view of spatial patterns that sees a field rather than a place phenomenon may better equip us to deal with the increasing afocality of urban life.

Of course, mere description is not enough; there is a pressing need in metropolitan planning for improved understanding of the determinants of the various dimensions of spatial structure. The most fruitful approaches to such theory appear to me to be those that seek to explain the locational behavior of various types of establishments, rather than those approaches that treat spatial structure as an aggregative system.[46] Yet the locational decision of each individual establishment is in some degree a function of the over-all spatial structure existing at the time of the decision; and, in turn, the consequence of thousands of individual locational decisions is an over-all spatial structure. For metropolitan planning purposes, then, we need a rigorously systematic way of describing over-all spatial structure and we need rigorously systematic theory which can help to predict the behavior of individual establishments.

The large metropolitan settlement is indeed the locus of

a wide variety of activities, and it does indeed comprise a more complex network of functional interdependencies than any one man can comprehend. I have also contended that many of the actors located within the settlement are participants in realms that far transcend the place-community, and that in playing out these roles they are not participants in the place-community at all. As users of locally provided goods and services, they *are* place-community members, however; and presumably their decision to locate in the metropolis represents, for each of them, an effort to find the location that offers the best opportunity for interaction with participants in all the realms in which they participate. The spatial structure of urban settlements and urban regions and the spatial structure of the urban realms are closely related; each is in some way a function of the other. Each resident in a large urban settlement who is a participant in high-level realms for a large proportion of his time presumably still finds the large concentrated settlement an advantageous locus for communicating with others at all realm levels. And yet, as I have indicated, there is a large amount of locational variation among participants in each realm; and the range of variation appears to be increasing rapidly.

The enlarged freedom to communicate outside one's place-community that the emerging technological and institutional changes promise, coupled with an ever-increasing mobility and ever-greater degrees of specialization, will certainly mean that urbanites will deal with each other over greater and greater distances. The spatial patterns of their interactions with others will undoubtedly be increasingly disparate, less and less tied to the place in which they reside or work, less and less marked by the unifocal patterns that marked cities in an earlier day.

It thus appears to me that the behavioral models, that would explain individual's locational decisions, and the descriptive models, that would portray over-all spatial structures of settlements and regions, would both profit from an orientation to communication patterns. If the previously stated proposition is valid, and settlements exist primarily as a reflection of men's efforts to increase opportunities for interaction, it then follows that both individual locational behavior and over-all spatial structure are mirrors of communications. With the changing patterns of communications that are imminent, then, we can expect that individuals' locations and that over-all spatial structures will also change—possibly in very dramatic ways.

There are large, though latent, opportunities for imaginative metropolitan plans to accommodate to these changes and to foster ease of intercourse. But metropolitan planners are not likely to keep abreast of these changes unless they are able to free themselves from the obsession with placeness and unless they can come to view the urban communities as spatially extensive, processual systems in which urbanites interact with other urbanites wherever they may be. For it is interaction, not place, that is the essence of the city and of city life.

NOTES

[1] Jesse Reichek, "On the Design of Cities," *Journal of the American Institute of Planners*, XXVII (May, 1961), 141-143. Ludwig von Bertalanffy, *Problems of Life, An Evaluation of Modern Biological and Scientific Thought* (New York: Harper & Bros., 1960), pp. 17 ff. See also Bertalanffy, "General System Theory," in *General Systems*, Yearbook of the Society for the Advancement of General Systems Theory, I (1956), pp. 1-10.

[2] Barclay Gibbs Jones has traced the origins of economic thought, concerned with city location and structure, back to the seventeenth century and finds essentially the same dominant conception throughout the development of the theory. "The Theory of the Urban Economy" (unpublished doctoral dissertation, University of North Carolina, 1960). The

idea of the city as a place occurs in the oldest preserved written statement on city planning, by Vitruvius, first century B.C.

[3] Hans Blumenfeld, "On the Concentric-Circle Theory of Urban Growth," *Land Economics*, XXV (May, 1949), 208-212; "The Tidal Wave of Metropolitan Expansion," *Journal of the American Institute of Planners*, XX (Winter, 1954), 3-14. United States Department of Commerce, *Future Development of the San Francisco Bay Area 1960-2020* (Washington: Government Printing Office, 1959).

[4] See the important commentary in N. S. B. Gras, *An Introduction to Economic History* (New York and London: Harper and Brothers, 1922), especially pp. 194-196. John R. P. Friedmann clearly presents the idea of the urban region in "The Concept of the Planning Region," *Land Economics*, XXXII (February, 1956), 1-13.

[5] See Rutledge Vining, "A Description of Certain Spatial Aspects of an Economic System," *Economic Development and Cultural Change*, III (no. 2), 147-195; John E. Brush, "The Hierarchy of Central Places in Southwestern Wisconsin," *The Geographic Review*, XLIII (No. 3, 1953); Ralph Edwin Birchard, "The Spatial Structure of the Oklahoma City Metropolitan Region." Unpublished Ph.D. dissertation, State University of Iowa, 1954.

[6] Walter Christaller, *Die Zentralen Orte in Suddeutchland* (Jena, 1933). An English language summary of Christaller's main ideas is contained in Vining, *op. cit.*, pp. 16-174. See also Allen K. Philbrick, "Principles of Areal Functional Organization in Regional Human Geography," *Economic Geography*, XXXIII (October, 1957), 299-336.

[7] See R. D. McKenzie, *The Metropolitan Community* (New York: McGraw-Hill Book Co., 1933), p. 352. Donald Bogue, *The Structure of the Metropolitan Community* (Ann Arbor: Horace H. Rackham, School of Graduate Studies, University of Michigan, 1950), p. 210.

[8] Walter Isard and others, *Methods of Regional Analysis: An Introduction to Regional Science* (New York: The Technology Press and John Wiley, 1960), pp. 677-678.

[9] Richard L. Meier, "The Measurement of Social Change," *Proceedings of the Western Joint Computer Conference*, 1959, 327-331; "Measuring Social and Cultural Change in Urban Regions," *Journal of the American Institute of Planners*, XXV (November, 1959), 180-190; *A Communication Theory of Urban Growth* (Cambridge: M.I.T. Press, 1962).

[10] "The Measurement of Social Change," p. 56.

[11] Albert Z. Guttenberg, "A Multiple Land Use Classification System," *Journal of the American Institute of Planners*, XXV (August, 1959), 143-150.

[12] For example, an establishment comprising a large corporate headquarters may house financial, marketing, sales, executive, service, and other activities that would be separately identified had each of these functions been separately housed or were each a separately owned administrative unit.

[13] See Meier, *op. cit.*; Britton Harris, "Some Problems in the Theory of Intraurban Location," *Operations Research*, IX (September-October, 1961), 695-721; Robert B. Mitchell, "The New Frontier in Metropolitan

Planning," *Journal of the American Institute of Planners*, XXVII (August, 1961), 169-175; John W. Dyckman, "The Changing Uses of the City," in "The Future Metropolis," *Daedalus* XC (Winter, 1961), 111-131; "An Examination of Metropolitan Plan-Making Strategy," *General Plan Laboratory Report*, Department of City and Regional Planning, University of California, Berkeley (January, 1961).

[14] Characterizing city planning as a social movement, as a governmental function, and as a technical profession, John T. Howard then summarizes the contemporary conception of the technical profession's substantive scope with classic precision: "The *focus* of the technical profession must be clearly understood as the physical form of urban and metropolitan environment. It is obviously concerned with the forces that shape the environment: physical, technological, social, economic; with evaluating the environment as it now exists in terms of its capacity to satisfy human needs; and with direct and indirect consequences of planned changes. The planner is also concerned with ways of bringing into being plans for environmental improvement—and with the political implementation of these plans. *But the plans themselves are plans of physical things.*" (Closing italics added.) "City Planning as a Social Movement, a Governmental Function, and a Technical Profession," Chapter 9 in Harvey S. Perloff, Ed., *Planning and the Urban Community* (Pittsburgh: Carnegie Institute of Technology and the University of Pittsburgh Press, 1961), p. 151.

[15] Mitchell and Rapkin define linkage as "the relationship between establishments characterized by continuing or frequently recurring interaction. Linkage leads to the movement of persons and goods between linked establishments and generates a tendency on the part of establishments so related to seek proximate locations or locations that are mutually accessible." *Urban Traffic: A Function of Land Use* (New York: Columbia University Press, 1954), p. 217. In a footnote on p. 111, they quote P. Sargant Florence in a passage in which he uses the term with approximately the same meaning, that linkage leads to proximity. They also quote Wroe Alderson (pp. 150-153) in a passage in which linkage is also used to imply a spatial relationship. John Rannells defines linkage more broadly, as "a relationship between establishments characterized by recurrent interactions which require movement of persons or of goods or the exchange of information." *Core of the City* (New York: Columbia University Press, 1956), p. 19. He then goes on to note that the network of an establishment's linkage is a strong force in determining its location. But for Rannells, as for me, linkage is a non-spatial concept. I am generalizing the concept still further than Rannells does, however, by deleting the requirement of recurrence of interaction. The strongest linkages and those having the greatest significance for social welfare may be the infrequent dependency ties.

[16] The term adapted spaces was introduced in Kevin Lynch and Lloyd Rodwin, "A Theory of Urban Form," *Journal of the American Institute of Planners*, XXIV (No. 4, 1958) 201-214; and in Kevin Lynch, "The Pattern of the Metropolis," in "The Future Metropolis," *Daedalus* XC (Winter, 1961), 79-98.

[17] Jean Fingerhut was approaching this idea of urbanity in her "Urbanity and the Physical Environment." Unpublished master's thesis, University of California, 1959.

[18] See, for example, Howard S. Lapin, "Index Numbers for Urban Travel," *Journal of the American Institute of Planners,* XXVII (August, 1961), 215.

[19] Meier, *A Communication Theory of Urban Growth, op. cit.;* Martin Meyerson, "Planning for Movement in Developing Countries," *Regional Planning* (United Nations Department of Economic and Social Affairs, 1959), pp. 85-93.

[20] See, for example, the testimony of James R. Rae, *Hearings before the Government Activities Subcommittee of the Committee on Government Operations,* House of Representatives, 87th Congress, First Session, November 29 and 30, 1961 (Washington, D.C.: U.S. Government Printing Office, 1962).

[21] Lynch identifies the adapted spaces as the voids between channels that "have in some way been modified to facilitate localized activities, whether by enclosure, improvement of the floor, manipulation of the shape, provision of fixed equipment, etc. This class includes such diverse objects as buildings, storage tanks, parking lots and vegetable gardens." Kevin Lynch, "A Classification System for the Analysis of the Urban Pattern." Unpublished manuscript, April 24, 1961.

[22] Cf. Foley's comment in his essay above, pp. 40-41.

[23] Guttenberg, *op. cit.*

[24] This important distinction was first brought to my attention by Harvey Leibenstein.

[25] Role and specialization level are probably closely related, and this becomes clear when each person's many roles are separately identified, as we shall see later. Since a man may play different roles at the same level of specialization, systematic classification for both characteristics is desirable.

[26] A great many scales have been developed, and new ones are being invented at a rapid rate now. See, for important examples, P. Sargant Florence's use of his location quotient for measuring localization in "Economic Efficiency in the Metropolis," in *The Metropolis and Modern Life,* R. M. Fisher, ed. (New York: Doubleday & Co., 1955), pp. 105-115; Britton Harris, *Industrial Land and Facilities for Philadelphia* (Philadelphia: Institute for Urban Studies of the University of Pennsylvania, 1956), in which degrees of dispersion and comparative movements of industrial groups are measured as functions of their centers of gravity and radii of gyration (pp. 138-140); Barclay Gibbs Jones, *op. cit., Part III,* in which a large array of measurements of central tendency are presented; Robert B. Reynolds, "Retail Specialization of Central Business Districts," *Journal of American Institute of Planners,* XXVI (November, 1960), 313-316; and John Q. Stewart and William Warntz, "Macrogeography and Social Science," *The Geographical Review,* XLVIII (No. 2, 1958), 167-184.

[27] Meier, "Measuring Social and Cultural Change in Urban Regions," *op. cit.*

[28] I am indebted to my former students, Paul Sedway, Samuel Dardick, and Edwin Fabrega for having clarified the definitions of centrality. *Studies in Metropolitan Planning,* Graduate Student Report, Department of City and Regional Planning, University of California, Berkeley, January, 1960, p. 27.

[29] The cartographatron developed by the Chicago Area Transportation Study is a device for preparing just this kind of map for trip data. See their Volume I, *Survey Findings,* December, 1959.

[30] Several such functional classifications of cities have been constructed. See, for examples, Victor Jones, "Economic Classification of Cities and Metropolitan Areas," *The Municipal Yearbook* (Chicago: International City Manager's Association, 1953); "A Service Classification of American Cities," P. Sargant Florence, *op. cit.;* and Howard Nelson, *Economic Geography,* XXXI (July, 1955), 189-210.

[31] In a brilliant treatise on the development of governmental ideology in the United States, Robert C. Wood has traced the origins of the place conceptions with uncommon clarity. *Suburbia: Its People and Their Politics* (Boston: Houghton-Mifflin, 1959).

[32] Herbert Gans found similar patterns among Boston's West Enders. See *The Urban Villagers* (New York: The Free Press of Glencoe, 1962). Marc Fried and Peggy Gleicher elaborate on this same phenomenon with detailed survey findings in "Some Sources of Residential Satisfaction in an Urban 'Slum,' " *Journal of the American Institute of Planners,* XXVII (November, 1961), 305-315.

[33] The word "field" has a spatial root, but it is commonly used in this nonspatial sense of an "area" of interest.

[34] It would be wrong to say "the town where he lives," for it is clear that in his various roles he *lives* in quite a range of other places. This man, unlike the janitor in his laboratory, lives throughout the world. This is a semantic matter of no trivial sort. The notion that a man lives where his house is located is fast becoming an anachronism from a less mobile era. Our population census has, as yet, found no way to overcome this vestigial bias.

[35] Meier, *op. cit.*

[36] There is no known way of measuring the "meaning" imbedded in messages. Only the amount of information they contain can be dealt with explicitly. At least for the present, we are limited to some type of highly aggregated index of informational volume, which might then be used as a gross indicator of levels of cultural wealth. For a general review of the recent state of communications theory, see Colin Cherry, *On Human Communications: A Review, a Survey, and a Criticism* (Cambridge: Technology Press of M.I.T., 1957).

[37] By this method of accounting, the larger the number of recipients of a given message, the larger the hubit income the population receives. This accords with our traditional conceptions of public education and with the high value we place upon popular access to the arts. The larger the audiences for books, theater, art, and news of current events, the richer is a population likely to be. The hubit does not account for the

ideational *quality* of the information that is received; only the number of units of information. A survey of the hubit income resulting from TV performances of *Hamlet* and of *I Love Lucy* would not seek to evaluate the relative literary merits of the two; it would seek only to estimate the number of bits of information presented by each and the average numbers of bits then absorbed by the TV audience. Of course, Hamlet transmits more content per minute than does Lucy, and a sensitive survey would account for that. Successive episodes of the Lucy show become highly redundant, so that a loyal follower experiences rapidly diminishing returns. This is less true of *Hamlet;* repeated viewings of the identical filmed performance would, for most receivers, continue to reveal content that was previously not absorbed. Here, too, of course, diminishing returns make subsequent performances less valuable for any single individual.

[38] It is apparent that almost everyone in the United States population today is a recipient of nationally distributed messages. As television viewer, magazine or newspaper reader, and as the consumer of products that incorporate innovations that arose in other parts of the country, he is beneficiary of world- and nation-realm activities. But he is not necessarily thereby also a participant in the world or national realms, for he may be acting in the role associated with the local realm.

Consider a child watching a television show seen over a national network. To the degree that he understands and is able to absorb the content of the messages coming through the television receiver, he cumulates hubits; but his role is likely to be no different from that played in watching a neighborhood puppet show. His self-image of his role, and hence his responses to the messages and his subsequent actions based upon them are unspecialized. In some degree, for him the TV is a part of his living room or of his neighborhood-based world.

A similar view is expressed by Morton Grodzins in his perceptive examination of the federal system, written for the President's Commission on National Goals. He contends that the typical congressman's self-image of role is as the representative of his home locale. Although he participates in the highest governmental council of the nation, insofar as he plays the role of lobbyist or servant for home-town interests he is not a member of the national realm. To the degree that he does play the role of national statesman serving the interests of the nation, he is then a participant in the national realm. I believe that, in much the same way, some representatives to metropolitan governmental councils from local city councils are playing the roles of protectors of home-town interests rather than those of metropolitan representatives.

In an allocation of man-hours to the various realms, then, we shall have to attempt somehow to allocate the proportions of time and the related proportions of hubits according to the individual's self-image of his roles.

[39] See, for example, Gunnar Alexandersson, *The Industrial Structure of American Cities—A Geographic Study of Urban Economy in the United States* (Stockholm: Almqvist & Wiksell, 1956).

[40] Henry Fagin, "Metropolitan Planning" (forthcoming); Robert B. Mitchell, *op. cit.*

[41] Some of the recent urban renewal organizations are difficult to classify in the traditional public or private boxes. The range of metropolitan organizations in Pittsburgh and the various downtown renewal groups, such as the Greater Baltimore Committee, are ostensibly nonpublic civic associations, but they perform the functions that city hall type of agencies perform in other cities and in quite the same manner.

[42] See Vining, *op. cit.*

[43] *Op. cit.*

[44] *Op. cit.*

[45] Parsons, Brinckerhoff, Hall, and Macdonald, *Regional Rapid Transit: A Report to the San Francisco Bay Area Transit Commission* (New York and San Francisco: Parsons, Brinckerhoff, Hall, and Macdonald, 1955).

[46] For some outstanding recent contributions to a behavioral theory, see Lowdon Wingo, Jr., *Transportation and Urban Land* (Washington, D.C.: Resources for the Future, Inc., 1961); Britton Harris, "Some Problems in the Theory of Intra-Urban Location," *op. cit.*; and John D. Herbert and Benjamin H. Stevens, "A Model for the Distribution of Residential Activity in Urban Areas," *Journal of Regional Science*, II (Fall, 1960), 21-36.

Public and Private Agents
of Change in Urban Expansion

William L. C. Wheaton

Metropolitan areas grow and take their peculiar form as the result of decisions to invest by public, private, and nonprofit agencies of widely varying types and the decisions to move by individuals, businesses, and others.

This essay analyzes the role of investment decisions in the processes of urban change. It seeks to demonstrate that investment decisions are not only widely dispersed geographically but are also made by widely varying types of institutions and individuals; public and private agencies; large, well-staffed agencies; and single individuals. The controlling criteria for these decisions are market facts or their absence, professional standards, and value judgments sometimes of a political nature. All of these criteria impinge upon most decisions, which therefore depend upon both a variety of criteria and concurrence by a variety of agents. In addition, current decisions are influenced by past decisions embodied in law, bureaucracy, administrative rules, or customary procedures. Neither private nor public systems of power can alter investment decision processes substantially, except under crisis conditions. If this view accurately reflects the forces influencing investment decisions affecting urban growth, then the modification or guidance of growth to achieve planned development patterns depends upon the provision of market data to those who decide, and the achievement of agreed-upon standards between the operative professions and bureaucracies. Metropolitan-area data services and metropolitan master plans would serve these purposes.

Before undertaking any further analysis of the agents or the processes of change, we ought to have some rough understanding of the kind of decisions being made and of the agencies who make them. Unfortunately, there has been no systematic analysis of this process and we can only piece together from fragmentary information a broad picture. Much of what we need to know must be inferred from construction statistics which are almost the only available data on the subject.

I. THE INVESTMENT MIX

Volumes and Types of Investment

Table I presents a summary of investment volumes made in the Pennsylvania part of the Philadelphia metropolitan area during a typical year in the late 1950's. The table is a first approximation containing some fairly obvious gaps in public investments receiving federal aid through state and special district channels. In an attempt to suppress the wide fluctuations which operate in any single category in any single year, the table is composed of averages of three or more years' investments. It gives, then, a breakdown of investments made by public and private agencies and by county areas within the Pennsylvania part of the Philadelphia metropolitan area. Tables II and III give percentage distributions by counties and for the region. Several aspects of the tables deserve emphasis. The first is the division of investments between public and private agencies. Table II indicates that this ratio varies widely from county to county. In Chester County, more than a third

Table I

Total Annual Public and Private Capital Outlay Expenditure, by Function, in the Five-County Philadelphia Metropolitan Area

(Averaged for period 1957-60)

(in thousands of dollars)

	Bucks	Chester	Delaware	Montgomery	Philadelphia	TOTAL
PUBLIC						
Federal[a]	—	—	—	—	$2,341	$2,341
State	$9,328	$10,396	$7,000	$10,687	$19,751	$57,162
Highways[b]	6,782	5,947	1,862	3,762	6,071	24,424
General State Authority[c]	920	2,759	2,104	1,130	8,010	14,923
State Hwy & Bridge Authority[d]	526	602	873	1,727	2,598	6,326
Supt. of Public Instruction[e]	1,100	1,088	2,161	4,068	3,072	11,489
Local government[f]	7,979	9,505	10,811	18,518	77,604	124,417
General capital expenditures	7,762	8,929	10,405	17,995	64,422	109,513
Education	5,512	7,033	7,854	13,094	16,000	49,493
Highways	405	564	709	1,394	9,148	12,220
Other general[g]	416	182	959	1,660	12,437	15,654
Utility expenditures	216	575	405	522	13,182	14,900
Total Public	17,307	19,901	17,811	29,205	99,696	183,920
PRIVATE						
Manufacturing[h]	48,463	13,903	27,731	62,097	126,656	278,850
Residential construction[i]	22,318	14,790	31,623	50,990	54,916	174,637
1 and 2 family	21,520	14,205	28,977	42,054	38,522	145,278
Other residential	798	585	2,646	8,936	16,394	29,359
Commercial[j]	3,882	1,666	6,421	12,745	17,993	42,707
New industrial building[j]	2,712	400	1,067	6,226	2,431	12,836
Other construction[k]	1,611	657	4,045	4,774	6,279	17,366
Additions, alterations & repairs[l]	4,595	2,292	7,822	10,068	21,468	46,245
Total Private	83,581	33,708	78,709	146,900	229,743	572,641
TOTAL PUBLIC AND PRIVATE	$100,888	$53,609	$96,520	$176,105	$329,439	$756,561

Source: See footnote no p. 157.

of investments were public, while in Montgomery County less than one-seventh were public. The average for the metropolitan area in these years was one-fifth public. This appears low when compared with national income accounts and historical statistics for other metropolitan areas. Indeed, the ratio of public investment to private investment appears to average between 40 per cent and 50 per cent and may exceed 50 per cent in central cities of major metropolitan areas and in communities heavily affected with defense or other public expenditures. National statistics may be slightly misleading in this respect because they combine expenditures made in urban areas with those made in rural or farm areas. It seems fair to presume that public expenditures are proportionately higher in the urban areas than they are in rural areas.

A second aspect of these tables demanding attention is the division of investment decisions between central and suburban areas. Less than half the total is in the central city in this instance, and, given the concentration of population growth during the last decade in the suburbs, this should be so in almost all metropolitan areas. It is noteworthy that the total

---

Sources of Table I   (Time periods vary):

a General Services Administration.
b Commonwealth of Pennsylvania, Department of Internal Affairs, *Pennsylvania Statistical Abstract 1961* (Harrisburg, Pa.: Bureau of Publications, September, 1961) Table 133, p. 161.
c Ibid. Table 136, p. 163.
d Ibid. Table 138, p. 165.
e Statistical Report of the Superintendent of Public Instruction, Harrisburg, for years 1956-57, 1957-58, and 1958-59.
f U.S. Department of Commerce, Bureau of the Census, *Local Government Finances in Standard Metropolitan Areas*, 1957, Census of Governments, Vol. III, No. 6 (Washington: GPO, 1959), Table 3, pp. 40-41.
g Ibid.
h Commonwealth of Pennsylvania, Department of Internal Affairs, *1960 Statistics by Major Industry Group for Counties and Urban Places*, 1960 Industrial Census of Pennsylvania (Harrisburg, Pa.: Bureau of Statistics, October, 1961), Release No. M-2-60.
i Commonwealth of Pennsylvania, Department of Labor and Industry, *Summary Building Operations in Pennsylvania* (Harrisburg, Pa.: Bureau of Research and Statistics, for the years 1957, 1958, 1959, and 1960). Estimated cost of building construction as reported on the permits.

New industrial building valuation was included because the statistics for "Manufacturing" exclude expenditures for establishments under construction.

Table II

Percentage Distribution of Annual Public and Private Capital Outlay Expenditure, by Function, Within Each of the Five Philadelphia Metropolitan Area Counties (1957-60)

	Bucks	Chester	Delaware	Montgomery	Philadelphia	TOTAL
PUBLIC						
Federal	—	—	—	—	0.7	0.3
State	9.2	19.4	7.3	6.1	6.0	7.6
Highways	6.7	11.1	1.9	2.1	1.8	3.2
General State Authority	0.9	5.1	2.2	0.6	2.4	2.0
State Hwy & Bridge Authority	0.5	1.1	0.9	1.0	0.8	0.8
Supt. of Public Instruction	1.1	2.0	2.2	2.3	0.9	1.5
Local government	7.9	17.7	11.2	10.5	23.6	16.4
General capital expenditures	7.7	16.7	10.8	10.2	19.6	14.5
Education	5.5	13.1	8.1	7.4	4.9	6.5
Highways	0.4	1.1	0.7	0.8	2.8	1.6
Other general	0.4	0.3	1.0	0.9	3.8	2.1
Utility expenditures	0.2	1.1	0.4	0.3	4.0	2.0
Total Public	17.2	37.1	18.5	16.6	30.3	24.3
PRIVATE						
Manufacturing	48.0	25.9	28.7	35.3	38.4	36.9
Residential construction	22.1	27.6	32.8	29.0	16.7	23.1
1 and 2 family	21.3	26.5	30.0	23.9	11.7	19.2
Other residential	0.8	1.1	2.7	5.1	5.0	3.9
Commercial	3.8	3.1	6.7	7.2	5.5	5.6
New industrial building	2.7	0.7	1.1	3.5	0.7	1.7
Other construction	1.6	1.2	4.2	2.7	1.9	2.3
Additions, alterations & repairs	4.6	4.3	8.1	5.7	6.5	6.1
Total Private	82.8	62.9	81.6	83.4	69.7	75.7
TOTAL PUBLIC AND PRIVATE	100.0	100.0	100.0	100.0	100.0	100.0

Derived from Table I

Table III

Percentage Distribution of Annual Public and Private Capital Outlay Expenditure, by Function, by County, for the Five-County Philadelphia Metropolitan Area (1957-60)

	Bucks	Chester	Delaware	Montgomery	Philadelphia	TOTAL
PUBLIC						
Federal	—	—	—	—	0.3	0.3
State	1.2	1.4	0.9	1.4	2.6	7.6
Highways	0.9	0.8	0.2	0.5	0.8	3.2
General State Authority	0.1	0.4	0.3	0.1	1.1	2.0
State Hwy & Bridge Authority	0.1	0.1	0.1	0.2	0.3	0.8
Supt. of Public Instruction	0.1	0.1	0.3	0.5	0.4	1.5
Local government	1.1	1.3	1.4	2.4	10.3	16.4
General capital expenditures	1.0	1.2	1.3	2.3	8.5	14.5
Education	0.7	0.9	1.0	1.7	2.1	6.5
Highways	0.1	0.1	0.1	0.2	1.2	1.6
Other general	0.1	—	0.1	0.2	1.6	2.1
Utility expenditures	—	0.1	0.1	0.1	1.7	2.0
Total Public	2.3	2.6	2.4	3.9	13.2	24.3
PRIVATE						
Manufacturing	6.4	1.8	3.7	8.2	16.7	36.9
Residential construction	2.9	2.0	4.2	6.7	7.3	23.1
1 and 2 family	2.8	1.9	3.8	5.6	5.1	19.2
Other residential	0.1	0.1	0.3	1.2	2.2	3.9
Commercial	0.5	0.2	0.8	1.7	2.4	5.6
New industrial building	0.4	0.1	0.1	0.8	0.3	1.7
Other construction	0.2	0.1	0.5	0.6	0.8	2.3
Additions, alterations & repairs	0.6	0.3	1.0	1.3	2.8	6.1
Total Private	11.0	4.5	10.4	19.4	30.4	75.7
TOTAL PUBLIC AND PRIVATE	13.3	7.1	12.8	23.3	43.5	100.0

Derived from Table I

investment is about 7 per cent of the estimated current value of investments in the region at the beginning of the period, which was a little over $11 billion. The Philadelphia rate was only 5 per cent, probably below replacement.

We might consider briefly the size of the individual decision package. Here the distinction must be made between new building decisions and investments in maintenance and repairs, alterations and enlargements, and replacement of equipment. Both new and replacement investments ultimately affect the form of the city. New buildings create new urban areas, expand others. Failure to maintain, repair, or replace ultimately leads to deterioration of buildings and their eventual abandonment; in the extreme it can lead to the depopulation of an urban area and the disappearance of a city. While one primary concern, in this paper, is with new investments, the larger and more identifiable other classes of investment are included in the tables and affect the size of decision.

If the average investment decision were valued at approximately $20,000, Table I suggests that 30,000 primary decisions to make new building investments were made during the typical year that this table reflects. Actually this number is probably too high and a closer figure might be around 20,000 new investment decisions plus 20,000 decisions on additions and repairs. In housing, for instance, roughly fifty decisions to build large housing projects may have accounted for nearly half of all the investment decisions involved. On the other hand, 3,000 to 4,000 individual homes were built to order by developers or contractors, involving an equal number of decisions.

The unit size of other decisions might be expected to be larger except for the fact that the table includes, under manufacturing, many decisions regarding plant and equipment as opposed to building. Permits for additions, alterations, and repairs, which are included, tend to run to rather small amounts, typically about $1,000 for residences and $7,000 for nonresidences. At the other end of the scale we have a few decisions regarding major highway improvements, major office or apartment buildings, or utility plants, ranging in size from $1 million to as large as $80 million. A few of these in any year could obviously make up a significant portion of total investments in a metropolitan area. The size range for Philadelphia public projects in a single year was from $28 million (subway extension) to $4,000 (paving parking lot), but this range excludes minor street and utility improvements. The size range for private investment was from $80 million (oil refinery) downward. In both classes a few dozen very large decisions apparently comprise as much as half the total. At the other end of the scale, there must be millions of individual decisions, regarding maintenance of buildings, for instance, which in the aggregate and over long periods of time affect the condition, and ultimately the form, of the city.

The size and competence of the agency making an investment decision is another area of interest. Here systematic data are almost wholly lacking. The City of Philadelphia with a capital budget of roughly $100 million per year is, over the years, the largest single decision agent, although less than half this amount is bona fide local expenditure, as is noted below. The General State Authority, which builds a large proportion of school buildings in Pennsylvania, and the Pennsylvania State Highway Department are also very large deciders. In some years major utilities like the Philadelphia Electric Company or the Bell Telephone Company may make decisions of major size and the aggregate of their smaller decisions always bulks large. With these exceptions, however, most investment decisions are made by business firms or gov-

Table IV

Number of Governmental Units by Type, Pennsylvania Part of Philadelphia Metropolitan Area, 1960

Number of Governmental Units

Constituent Unit	Total	School	County	Town-ship	Mun. of 1,000+	Mun. of 1,000−	Special District
Bucks County	108	54	1	31	12	10	0
Chester County	146	72	1	57	11	5	0
Delaware County	100	48	1	21	24	4	2
Montgomery County	130	66	1	38	19	5	1
Philadelphia	3	1	0	0	1	0	1
TOTAL	487	241	4	147	67	24	4

ernment agencies which only intermittently make large investment decisions and by a still larger number of others whose decisions are always small and intermittent.

The same is true of other local government agencies, whose aggregate volume of building is substantial. Outside of the City of Philadelphia there are nearly 500 units of local government in the four-county area, including townships, towns and cities, counties, school boards, and special districts. Some of these make decisions only once every four or five years and only a few of them are regularly in the business of making decisions to build. Tables IV and V give the types of local government units and the population sizes served by them.

Table V

Population Served by General Governmental Units in Philadelphia Metropolitan Area, 1960

Population Size

County	1,000 or less	1,001 to 2,500	2,501 to 5,000	5,001 to 10,000	10,001 to 25,000	25,001 to 50,000	50,001 to 100,000	100,000 or more
Bucks	16	21	10	4	3	—	—	—
Chester	31	24	13	2	3	—	—	—
Delaware	5	10	13	12	6	1	2	—
Montgomery	7	21	17	10	4	3	—	—
Philadelphia	—	—	—	—	—	—	—	1
TOTAL	59	76	53	28	16	4	2	1

It will be noted that there are more than 100 units of government in each of the suburban counties, and that roughly half of these serve populations of less than 5,000. If we now refer to Table I and divide any suburban category by 50 or some similar number, the average value of decisions being reached in a local government area is comparatively small, and the fraction of metropolitan total is invariably below 1 per cent, and usually a tiny fraction thereof.

In both the public and the private fields we have the categories of "aided" and "unaided" or independent decisions. "Aided" decisions refers to those in which another agent contributes funds or exercises controls, so that this "aider" becomes influential in the decisions. A public-aided decision is one in which another agency of government provides loans,

Table VI

Summary of the 1959-1964 Capital Program by Source of Funds
City of Philadelphia

(In ooo's of dollars)

Source	Total	1959	1960	1961	1962	1963	1964
Federal............	$119,881	11,084	18,978	30,164	24,439	20,390	14,826
State..............	363,165	24,870	49,995	50,000	160,009	26,450	51,850
Railroad..........	1,260	—	1,260	—	—	—	—
Township.........	675	550	—	—	25	—	100
Assessments.......	16,800	2,950	2,810	2,750	2,750	2,750	2,750
Industrial Redevelopment Funds....	2,000	500	500	1,000	—	—	—
Total—Other than City funds.......	503,781	39,954	73,543	83,914	187,214	49,630	69,527
Operating revenue..	24,597	3,784	3,997	4,219	4,188	4,248	4,161
Self-sustaining loan.	130,600	12,044	23,615	33,661	30,137	16,153	14,990
Loan subject to debt limit.............	148,120	22,086	26,165	33,740	21,946	22,481	21,701
Available loan funds	13,446	12,446	1,000	—	—	—	—
Total—City Funds .	316,764	50,360	54,777	71,620	56,272	42,882	40,853
GRAND TOTAL..	$820,545	90,314	128,320	155,534	243,485	92,512	110,379

Totals may not add due to rounding.
Source—Philadelphia Capital Budget, 1959-64.

grants, or other forms of aid to assist a local government. State grants for school construction and state and federal grants for highway construction are examples in the public field. In Philadelphia 60 per cent of the current six-year capital budget is state or federal aided and for 1962 the ratio is 73 per cent. Table VI gives an indication of the magnitude and variation of aids. In the private field we have something quite similar operating where banks make mortgage loans to private builders and investors, and we have, of course, a mixed category wherein government agencies extend loans, grants, or guarantees to private agencies. In many areas a few lenders of large size make half or more of all mortgage loans. They obviously exercise much influence. In all of these classes of aided decisions to invest, the private or public agency making the grant or loan has a very substantial voice in the ultimate decision and may have special competence or skill in making decisions of this type. We will return to this theme later.

Controlling Criteria of Decision

What types of criteria guide each of the several classes of decisions to build? It becomes obvious immediately that investment decisions may be divided between those determined largely by market or by nonmarket criteria. Residential construction is largely market determined. Few builders can afford to build large quantities of homes in locations which customers do not prefer. The location and size of stores and shopping centers are dictated within very narrow limits by the number, income, and buying habits of the customers available in the surrounding market area. The location and size of elementary schools are almost completely determined by the number of school-age children already living in the area and not yet in schools, or temporarily attending already overcrowded ones. Utility lines, streets and major thoroughfares, and other classes of public construction are controlled within narrow limits by the same market determinants. It is rare that either public or private agencies make major errors in the location of such facilities. The customers are usually there, and merely have to be counted.

The number and character of investment decisions based on other than market criteria are somewhat limited. A national manufacturing firm seeking to locate a new plant usually has a choice among several metropolitan areas and often has a choice among a substantial number of alternative sites within any metropolitan area. The location of a regional office for a national manufacturer or distributor is similarly often free of narrowly defined limits. The location of an electric generating plant or an electric utility will be affected more strongly by the availability of water and sources of fuel than it will be by the location of the customers. The location of new colleges and universities, research laboratories, regional offices of federal agencies, federal defense installations, and a few other categories of building may be relatively free of customer-oriented determinations.

Upon the generous presumption that one-half of federal construction, one-eighth of highways, one-quarter of other state expenditures, one-quarter of education, one-third of utility construction, one-half of new industrial building, and one-half of other construction are locationally free of market determinants, somewhat less than 5 per cent of all the investments shown on the table would be locationally free. If these very crude estimates understate the facts by 100 per cent, we are still dealing with less than 10 per cent of the total of capital outlay expenditures in a metropolitan area. The non-market-oriented locational decisions are subject to a wide variety of other criteria. Some of them are almost purely political in character, as when the federal government makes a decision to locate a major laboratory facility in the state of a distinguished senator who happens to be chairman of a key committee. Others may be highly personal, as when a major industrial leader, whose home is in a certain city, decides to make a major plant expansion in that city without serious consideration of the economic advantages of other possible locations. Others of these decisions may be guided by technical determinants—the availability of cooling water in the case of the electric power plants or the availability of a reservoir of scientific personnel for a laboratory.

In these last remarks we have obviously been referring to two categories of locational decisions. First is the macroscale where we are considering whether or not a facility goes into a metropolitan area or, within the metropolitan area, whether the location will be central or suburban. There is, however, another scale—the microscale—wherein the decision is to locate a facility at this specific location or at another location a half mile away or perhaps two miles away. At the microscale—and this is the scale at which decisions are made which vitally affect the economic efficiency and particularly the amenity of the metropolitan area—other types of consideration enter into the locational decision. These are what may be called pseudoscientific, professional, or customary criteria. These may be of considerable importance to the structure and growth of the metropolitan area. If mortgage lenders generally regard North Philadelphia as a bad investment area because of the occupants' race, the condition of the buildings, or for other reasons, this belief will largely determine the character and extent of the investments in that area regardless of the objective facts and only the most extraordinary measures will produce new investment in such areas. In Minneapolis, investments north and east of certain streets are taboo among mortgage lenders, and it follows that in considerable degree they are not made; beyond a line circumscribed by a five- or six-mile radius of City Hall, residential developments were regarded as "too far out," and so, for a number of years, mortgage loans were not made beyond this boundary line. Only when a builder secured outside capital to provide mortgage loans for what subsequently became the largest development in the area did mortgage lenders recognize that loans outside this boundary line were not taboo.

Similar considerations operate in many other fields. Recreation leaders believe in certain kinds of playgrounds and further believe that certain facilities should be located within a quarter-mile walking distance of users. Responsive to these beliefs, standards are established by planning agencies and playgrounds are located as if these were the most important criteria. Educational leaders have standards for the minimum size of schools and maximum distance of schools from their customers, the students. Though these standards are in conflict, the latter are almost universally sacrificed to the former in current practice. Mr. Conant has engaged in a national campaign to assure the public and educationists that a high school of a certain size is essential to the provision of decent education at that level, even if it means that students shall travel an hour by bus to their destination each morning.[1] Highway locations and capacities are determined by engineering criteria based on engineers' impressions of how people will behave under certain circumstances, despite some evidence to the contrary. Most zoning ordinances are based upon the belief that the ordinance will regulate the density and character of land use, despite overwhelming evidence that this is not so. Many private investment decisions are based upon the same illusion despite the same facts.

Fact and Value in Market Decisions

As has already been suggested, market criteria, in the sense of the location and behavior of consumers, are the decisive force affecting as much as 90 per cent of the microlocational decisions to invest in metropolitan areas. If we examine housing market decisions—and these are one of the largest single categories affecting metropolitan growth—we will observe that both the developer and the lender are largely guided by the conviction that customers will show up for a particular type of housing at a particular location. The whole behavior of developers of suburban shopping centers and individual operators of retail stores is affected by similar considerations. The practitioners in both these fields, to the extent that their practice is systematic, analyze the number of customers, their income, and their relative distance from competing locations and estimate the potential number that may be attracted to a particular residential or commercial development. In some cases the procedures of analysis are comparatively sophisticated, based on recent behavior of people and utilizing current data sources. In other cases the decision process is more or less intuitive, based upon recent personal experience or just plain hunch. By and large, these decision processes produce an acceptable quality of decision. A few residential developments have failed to sell. A few shopping centers have gone through the wringer; but by and large, private investments have produced profits, and few shareholders have asked whether profits might have been larger at other locations or with other types of facilities.

If, however, we examine the state of the data upon which market-oriented decisions are made, the actual state of knowledge of those who make decisions ostensibly based on market criteria, and the state of understanding of those who advise on these decisions, we get a very different picture. Market decisions have a fact component, a judgment component, and a value component which are fairly readily distinguishable. The fact questions relate to the number of potential users for a particular facility in the market at the time of the decision. How many school children are there in a district? How many drivers now wish to drive from A to B each morning? How many buyers of what income live within the normal driving distance of a shopping-center location? How many families are in the market this year for new single detached houses priced at $16,000? Each of these questions is, within narrow limits, subject to fairly objective determination. The judgments involved in market decisions include judgments regarding the continuity of present trends, i.e., the stability of behavior observed in the past, judgments of the comparative advantage of one product or location as opposed to another product or location, and judgments concerning the discount rates, interest rates, or yield rates which justify an investment in a particular location or product or process.

Finally, there are value decisions which public agencies make in the form of decisions to invest in schools as opposed to hospitals, or playgrounds as opposed to highways, and which businessmen make to invest in one endeavor or another where the profit opportunities are approximately equal. In both public and private decisions, time preferences play an important role in this value area.

What is striking about decisions at this level is that the fact component of decisions is very often weak, inadequate, or nonexistent. Most decision-makers usually do not have access to the controlling facts. Only the largest, the best staffed, or the most alert of deciders, public or private, can obtain them or know how to use them. Thus mortgage lenders in the residential building field typically finance houses without knowing how many houses are being put under construction, without an awareness of the income, tenure, or home-buying propensities of the families in the market, and ignorant of the number of homes presently on the market and unsold, or the number of apartments presently on the market and vacant. Most mortgage lending and most residential building is undertaken on the basis of hunch, intuitive feel of the market, and experience with last year's product in last year's location.

These tend to make producer responses to changes in taste very slow and incremental. Similar situations prevail in many other fields, in smaller commercial investments, in smaller plant location decisions, in almost all the decisions of small units of local government, the characteristic type of government in areas where most of the growth occurs.

Quite opposite conditions obtain among many classes of decisions made by larger decision-makers. Major utility companies, large commercial investors, and central city governments are usually quite well staffed, have some research facilities, and take the pains to acquire the facts relevant to the decision at hand. Even these agencies, of course, have to make judgments concerning the continuity or discontinuity of observed current trends. That the possibility of error is large is indicated, for instance, by the Ford Motor Company's experience with the Edsel car. Nevertheless, these larger decision-makers probably rarely make mistakes, and certainly rarely because of the absence of facts relevant to the decisions.

These agencies may make mistakes in the sense that they fail to recognize market opportunities because the market information they assemble is fragmentary and ad hoc rather than systematic. A few years ago, one of the largest food chains in the Philadelphia area, for instance, a capital gain operation from start to finish, systematically analyzed the market for chain food stores in the Philadelphia region. They found enough underserviced areas to enable them to program the opening of a new store each month for five years. At the end of the five-year period they were still short of exhausting the profitable opportunities. Their stores had an average annual sales volume per unit of well over twice that of their competitors, and the half dozen men involved have each become many times a millionaire. It would appear that their competitors were grossly negligent in their systematic appraisal of the market opportunities as compared with this firm.

A few years ago the Philadelphia Chamber of Commerce made a survey of the market analysis practices of the fifty largest firms in the Philadelphia metropolitan area. At the end of the survey the members of the committee, businessmen and market analysts with some of the most advanced firms, had a clear idea of why their enterprises were profitable and making money was so easy. The lack of market information and the absence of personnel devoted to market analysis in most firms was, by and large, quite striking.

Decision Chains and Nonmarket Criteria

Both market and nonmarket-oriented decisions involve the cooperation of numerous parties, public and private, who must participate in almost any venture. Each of these participants has criteria, whether they be formal or not, which guide its participation. Thus the public or private initiator of an investment proposal must follow a sequence of tests and checks, to ensure that all of the other participants will cooperate, in what degree, or subject to what limitations. This leads to a sequence of decisions, which we may call a "decision chain." If any major link in the chain fails or cannot be modified, the venture cannot proceed. In these tests and checks, and in securing cooperation, professional technicians, architects, engineers, lawyers, appraisers, public administrators and the like are the major actors, as agents for other principals. Their role may be decisive in securing a complete chain of decision, or in frustrating it.

Listed below are some, at least, of the steps involved in reaching what I call a primary decision to build. For convenience I have chosen some of the steps which a residential developer goes through in deciding to proceed with a typical, modest-sized residential subdivision.

I. Background knowledge, preconditions to initiation
   A. The state of the housing market, i.e., price classes and sales rates
   B. The state of the mortgage market, i.e., the availability and cost of funds
   C. Construction costs
   D. General information on land prices and availability
   E. General information on the state of regulation, taxes, and community services in the market area

II. Exploratory studies or analyses
   A. Comparison of the cost and suitability of alternative sites
   B. Pricing of the most favorable sites
   C. Preliminary check with the lender on the suitability of the site selected
   D. Preliminary check on zoning of the site selected
   E. Preliminary check on subdivision code affecting the site selected
   F. Preliminary check on the building code affecting the site selected
   G. Preliminary inquiry with site engineer or landscape architect regarding cost of site development
   H. Preliminary check with architect or general or subcontractor on modifications of building plan
   I. Check with potential general subcontractors on current costs and prices and on costs of potential modifications of building plans
   J. Preliminary check with sources of front money or equity capital

III. Tentative decision to go ahead
   A. Optioning of site
   B. Retention of landscape architect for site planning
   C. Review and first approval by sponsor of subdivision plan

D. Submission of subdivision plan to the city
E. Submission of streets plan to city engineer
F. Check with water company regarding service connections
G. Check with sewer department regarding outfall requirements
H. Check with local utility regarding power availability at the site
I. Submission of subdivision plan to FHA
J. Retention of architect for preparation of house plans
K. Review and first approval of house plans by sponsor
L. Submission of preliminary plans to mortgage lender
M. Submission of FHA insurance application to mortgage lender
N. Submission of detailed plans to potential syndicate or partnership members
O. Drafting of syndicate or partnership agreement
IV. Primary decision to invest
A. to O. Repeat for final agreements

It will be noted that only if all of these steps and many others, not enumerated, produce affirmative acceptable answers it is possible for the primary decision to invest to be made. If any of the requirements to be met produce negative answers, unforeseen requirements, requirements for modification, change or the like, the project may at least be delayed, most certainly be modified, and possibly may be dropped entirely. Once the primary decision has been made to go ahead, it is still possible for the project to fall by the wayside if subsequent precise plans do not meet the requirements of any of the parties involved, or the plan may have to be modified to meet the requirements of any of a score of agents. It is obvious that before a bit of dirt is moved a hundred or more steps, tests, and agreements must be taken.

There is one other aspect of each of these steps in the chain of decisions leading to investments which deserve some amplification. If we examine any of these steps in detail, we will find that it involves decisions at several levels by the participants involved or their agents. Let us take step III-C as an example. Here the developer has tentatively selected a site which he has tentatively reviewed with his site engineer or landscape architect. Both parties think that the site is developable in such a way as to produce a reasonable cost per lot, generally meeting the requirements of the city's subdivision ordinance, the zoning ordinance, the sanitary code, the standards of the municipal streets department, the fire department, and so forth.

The engineer or landscape architectural firm consulted, however, must render this general knowledge specific to the site and test each of these features in detail in the preparation of a specific plan. For these purposes the matter will usually be referred to a technician or a professional person at a junior level who is expected to prepare detailed plans, run grades, utility lines, sketch out the plot lines, compute lot sizes, estimate—first in a crude way and later in detail—costs of cut and fill, costs of installing utilities, and the like. This technician operates in the light of knowledge concerning what he believes to be the controlling technical standards required by his own professional code and training and what he believes to be the standards controlling others in the decision chain, i.e., the municipal planning commission, streets department, utility department, and the like, and the state of the market.

When a detailed plan has been developed it is first submitted to the principal in the engineering or landscape firm and then by him to the sponsor. At either stage, the plan may be revised to meet slightly different expectations, standards, or market judgments or design judgments of either party. Note that, in this process, fact, judgments, technical standards, and market judgments have been operative not merely with respect to what is actually known by the technician involved but also with respect to what others may think, believe, or utilize as operating standards, others to whom the plan will have to be submitted and whose approval it must obtain.

It is because of the interdependence of decisions and their simultaneous dependence upon fact, technical standards, the appraisal of others regarding the relevant facts, and market, aesthetic and other judgments, that the decision-making chain is both so complicated and at the same time so highly dependent on custom or usage. None of the actors involved in these steps can act effectively unless most of the time he is making reasonably accurate judgments concerning the probable behavior of many other parties in the transaction. If he is frequently in error, he will shortly be out of business. If he proposes anything radically new or different, he will burden his sponsor or principal with untold complications and the possibility of a turndown by the municipality, the banker, the contractors, or ultimately the market. These facts obviously give a very conservative cast to all decisions made at every level; and they emphasize the importance that professional standards and criteria have in the development and decision-making chain.

II. THE PLURALISM OF METROPOLITAN DECISIONS

Public Decision Processes and Institutions

Almost all investment decisions today require approval or cooperation by public agencies. The instrumentalities for public decision-making with respect to urban development should also be analyzed by the magnitude of the development decisions they make or act upon. Reference has already been made to the size of local suburban government units in the

Philadelphia area. It will be noted that only sixteen government units serve 10,000 or more people, four serve 25 to 50,000, and only two serve more than 50,000. Thus, in effect, only six of these government jurisdictions are in a position to employ full-time planning services and, in fact, only one does do so. Out of the four counties, two have excellent planning staffs serving local government units as well as the county, one has a full-time staff of indifferent quality, and one has no full-time staff. These are very crude measures of the size and competence of the governments making development decisions and we can only make some broad inferences with respect to the quality of the development decisions being undertaken by these units of government.

The growing literature in political decision-making by local governments gives us some insights into the competence of these units to make development decisions affecting the metropolitan area. Local elected officials are predominately part-time public servants, involved primarily in their private business activities, and with little *expertise* in government. In addition, they tend to be people who are local in origin, rooted deeply in the traditions and economic circumstances of the past. These characteristics in some respects have poorly equipped them for the vastly different decisions of the present. When the Levitt concern moved into Falls Township in Bucks County, with its proposal to build a city of 15,000 homes, the township was governed by a group of local farmers whose total governmental decisions in the preceding decade had involved the building of a small culvert, a short strip of country road, the addition of a toilet to a school, and the like. Yet these were the people in charge of a government of an area in which there were to be built 300 miles of streets, sewers and water lines, and $500 million worth of public and private buildings.

In addition, studies of the behavior of political leaders in local government suggest that they are strongly indisposed toward the making of decisions involving conflict within the community. Case after case analyzing local development decisions reveals public officials seeking to avoid making tough decisions, to avoid confronting issues before it is absolutely necessary to confront them, and, where decisions must be made, to defer to "experts" or to other levels of government or to delegate responsibility to nongovernmental groups which can reach some sort of a consensus. Local government is particularly sensitive to pressures from local groups. Development decisions often involve threats—either to the property rights of some residents or, more dangerously, to their image of the community in which they live. Either kind of threat is likely to evoke the most impassioned responses from directly affected factions of the population. Local elected officials are poorly equipped to respond to these pressures. They must necessarily value the current applied pressures more highly than the less specific sentiments of the rest of the public or the long-run needs of the community. Their very tenure in office depends upon such an evaluation. Only within narrow limits do they have the possibility or the power to delegate decision-making to others less vulnerable to local particularisms and short-term concerns.

As a consequence of these characteristics of the public decision-making process large numbers of urgently needed decisions are put off indefinitely. Major highway decisions in almost every metropolitan area may take as long as ten years to resolve, where local groups come into conflict with local, county, or state highway officials in controversies about the alignment of such facilities. The acquisition of sites for future schools and parks is frequently deferred until it is too late to buy such sites at reasonable prices. Zoning and subdivision control tend to be manipulated to preserve a past image of a rural community even when it is in the process of rapid conversion to a densely developed urban area.

Four methods of resolving local development controversies appear to be prevalent. In a few instances local political leaders develop convictions about what is to the best interest of the community. They lay their political fortunes on the line and, as often as not, are defeated in the next election if they seriously attempt to stand up for what they regard as the community welfare. Such cases are rare, but frequent enough to induce a broad measure of caution in other elected officials. In a second and more common class of case, the local officials defer to the judgment of technical experts or higher levels of government. In this class of case, which is particularly characteristic of highway decisions, local officials take the position that the need for a highway or the need for a certain alignment is a technical matter and the engineers have settled it. Or they may say, "It is for the state to decide," or the state and the federal government, and, "We cannot interfere with the decision." In some cases local officials will initially accept responsibility for a decision. Later, when the heat gets too great, they will defer to the technical character or the superior level of government responsible for the decision. In a third class of cases, local officials seek to achieve consensus by referring decisions to citizen groups and organizations in a position to reach an accommodation at least among activists. Here the technique is to appoint a representative citizen group which has some built-in reflection of the community tensions, but is loaded in favor of what appears to be the least dangerous solution. Such committees are made responsible for reconciling conflicts within the community, developing an accommodation which will minimize antagonisms within the community, and suppressing or appeasing the opposition. When the group has come up with its compromise, public officials ratify and enforce it. In the fourth class of case the decision is never made. It is postponed indefinitely, or until mounting demands for action force a solution through one of the mechanisms described above.

In larger government units very similar processes prevail. Even the largest cities have had considerable difficulty in making decisions regarding the alignment of expressways, the location of public housing projects, the location and character of urban renewal projects, the development of new shopping centers, and the adoption of modern zoning ordinances. The case studies of decision-making in these larger cities suggests that here, too, with rare exceptions, mayors are rarely willing to lay their political fortunes on the line to reach a decision which they may recognize as necessary for the public welfare. More commonly they will make all decisions which do not involve controversy and seek to avoid making, or to avoid responsibility for making, decisions which involve controversy regarding the future of the area. In such larger cities the use of civic groups to reconcile conflicting pressures and to achieve accommodations is almost universal, and postponement for months and often years—occasionally decades—is common. Philadelphia has debated the alignment of the Delaware Expressway for more than a decade. New York has debated the expressway across downtown Manhattan for about thirty years. The cost of these delays are not easy to calculate precisely but they certainly are enormous.

Past and Present Decisions

At this point it is necessary to distinguish between past decisions and issues and current decisions and issues. Most of the body of public policy was decided at some time in the past, often in the remote past. At the time that these issues were bruited, the then coalitions of power and influence reached some kind of an accommodation which was adopted and built into public policy. Thus decisions to engage in welfare programs were largely adopted in the thirties. The decision to pave streets was adopted in the 1890's. The decision to base local government revenues primarily on the property tax was decided over a period of about a hundred years during the eighteenth and nineteenth centuries. At the time that such a decision is made there may be a considerable amount of tugging and pulling and community controversy regarding the basic policy and issues. But once the decision was made, and expressed in law or other public policy, its implementation was turned over to some bureaucracy or group of experts who were then armed with the power to carry out the policy at some minimal level.

There may be recurring minor-level controversies regarding the extent to which a policy is to be implemented, but such controversies usually arise in a general competition for tax or private resources, as in budget hearings and the like. Ultimately, decisions regarding the level of an activity tend to accumulate through time as a result of slow steady growth and evolving pressures and political leaders' responses to the popularity or unpopularity of the basic policies involved. Thus, at any one time, we find that the recreation policy of a city is pretty much a settled matter. A playground will be bought each year and 2.3 per cent of the budget of the city will be devoted to servicing playgrounds and providing leadership. If even a considerable number of citizen groups interest themselves in the subject of recreation, they may be able to increase the budget for acquisition or service by 1 or 2 per cent, at the expense of some other program, but this is the range of choice available to them without extraordinary consensus and extraordinary effort. As a consequence, lower level efforts are expended by the groups especially interested in this subject, but the basic decisions have been made and are a matter of settled policy embodied in institutions and processes.

Changes in basic policy arise as a result of crises. A dramatic event or a slowly accumulating basketful of problems in a particular subject matter area may precipitate widespread community controversy, the organization of coalitions of interest groups, the development of a new policy and its adoption and embodiment in bureaucracy. But even so great a national debate as that over the establishment of urban renewal policies did not lead to intense controversy in most of the major cities of the country. It was adopted by common consent because it was recognized that there was a need for public and private action and that, within the general policy framework proposed, there would be room for negotiation and compromise; that there would be some joint rewards for both public and private groups; and that there might be competition between private groups for the sharing of specific rewards.

Crisis appears in specific decisions when a general program which is a matter of settled policy comes into conflict with intensely felt values of local groups or vital economic interests of some business. Thus, specific highway and redevelopment decisions may become matters of local crisis where major projects are involved which impose costs—either emotional or economic or political—upon segments of the community which those segments are unwilling or are unable to tolerate. But note that the controversy here is within the frame of reference of a generally accepted public policy and falls within the domain of a bureaucracy, a professional group, or a set of processes which are otherwise proceeding in their routine work. Such controversies are likely to be heavily influenced by the accustomed processes of the bureaucracies involved.

The character of these controversies is segmental and particular rather than general. There is a general policy to provide express highways. The technicians have said that a highway is needed to the northeast and have proposed an alignment. The mayor and the council agree that this selection accords with their general sense of priorities. The controversy will arise because five neighborhood groups, two churches, ten stores, and four manufacturers are threatened by the destruction or division of their neighborhood by the highway alignment. These groups will coalesce, form a combat force, succeed in blocking the proposed alignment—in effect, succeed in pushing it to the east or the west, out of their area of interest and into the area of concern of other comparable groups. These groups in turn will organize to combat the new menace and the community is faced with a decision, within the framework of settled policy, as to which group will be adversely affected by what is commonly recognized to be needed in the public welfare.

On more general policies, e.g., on the controversy between highways and transit, particular organized groups—central-property owners, railroads, transit interests, and the like—may be able to achieve their objectives without city-wide controversy, particularly if they are at pains to reach accommodations with competing interests, such as automobile users, in advance of staking out their claims. Where controversies do arise, the previously described procedures for resolution become operative, and in these procedures accommodation is reached, usually with technical assistance.

Private Systems of Power

Hunter and his followers have made much of the theory that private networks of power and influence make most public decisions.[2] The studies of most other students demonstrate that this is rarely the case. In most cities there is no monolithic structure of power, pyramidal in shape, with a few influentials at the top making basic decisions for both the private and the public sectors of the economy. Rather there is a multiplicity of lesser concentrations of power, relatively independent of each other, competing for influence at times and in certain subject-matter areas, cooperating at other times and in other subject-matter areas, occasionally engaged in outright conflict, and often used by political leaders to reconcile tensions and conflicts within the community. Political institutions should be viewed as a part of this system of power and influence, which is in constant flux.

The city's systems of influence or power are composed of constellations or concentrations of power and influence based upon economic, business, or political or civic interests. These may be headed by bankers, professional or industrial leaders, or by civic or political leaders. They are organized around business, nationality, religious, political, or civic interests. Each is a small network of communication and influence tied together by daily business or political relationships or other less formal common interests. Few of these constellations have across-the-board interests in local affairs. Some of them are interested in the business world and things affecting business. Others are concerned with particular problems: urban renewal, highways, housing, taxation, or in some such subject as health or welfare. Few of these groups are closed. Most of them are open to the admission of newcomers in varying degrees and at different times.

Few of these groups have constant relationships with other similar groups. The relationships may vary from competitive to cooperative, depending upon time, circumstances, and the subject at hand. On the other hand there are "natural" coalitions which may operate recurringly on a variety of subjects where the common interests of one constellation coincide frequently with the common interests of another constellation. Communication between the groups is intermittent though communication within any group may be regular. These communication flows tend to reinforce the solidity and the effectiveness of the group under conditions of what Deutsch[3] calls joint rewards. Information flows along these channels of communication—information which is often bad or in-adequate but which evokes responses.

The perception of interest varies from group to group and from time to time. Groups may have an interest in the subject and not recognize it, or they may have no interest in the subject and believe that they do have. Even where a group feels it has an interest in the subject matter, it may be unable to mobilize its members quickly enough to exercise its potential influence on the event; or it may evaluate the situation as one in which it is not likely to be influential and it may, therefore, prefer to remain inactive rather than to run the risk of taking a position and losing. Finally, since we are discussing metro-politan growth, it should be noted that most constellations of influence and power have some sort of a geographic locus. They may be interested in central city or local suburban affairs, but they are rarely interested in both. They may be interested in the problems of a part of a city but not all of it. There are geographic overlaps and geographic gaps in the areas of concern of each of the constellations involved.

This broad picture of the institutions of power and influ-ence conforms, I believe, to that provided by Robert Dahl, Charles Adrian, Morris Janowitz, Edward Banfield, Wallace Sayre, Robert Wood, and other students of the subject.[4] I am not seeking to introduce any new material here but rather to summarize my reading of that literature.

Decision-Making in the Mixed Economy

Now let us return to our original theme, decision-making regarding metropolitan development. If we analyze the proc-esses through which these institutions of private and public power make decisions regarding the growth of the metro-politan area, do we find any guiding principles? Hunter and his followers, and conspiracy theorists of business, argue that there are, in fact, a limited number of highly influential people who make basic decisions and are the directing force behind public and private policy. Economic theorists, from Adam Smith down, argue that the invisible hand of the market is the dominating force and that its mechanisms automatically dictate the behavior of the several participants. The managerial-revolution theorists like Burnham contend that the decisions are in the hands of key technicians.[5] Traditional political theory assumes the decisions are in the hands of elected officials and political machines. Dahl and his followers argue, on the other hand, that an examination of the process of decision-making in urban areas indicates that no such coordination exists and that the processes are in fact autonomous, or only tangentially influence one another. In this view, a combination of the private market, specialized interest groups, business combinations, political machines, and civic leaders —each operating within a limited subject matter framework and a limited geographic area—in fact make the operating decisions.

It is my conviction that only the latter group of analysts are in touch with reality and are accurately describing the conditions as they exist in typical metropolitan areas in the United States. It is true that in Pittsburgh there is a considerable concentration of power and that a half dozen people around a table at the Duquesne Club can make some classes of major decisions. In Philadelphia or New York or Boston, however, even a hundred people around a similar table could not reach decisions on matters of very wide significance. It is also true that the Duquesne Club group can make decisions only as they affect a very limited subject-matter area. Under Mr. Hunter's analysis, Mr. Mellon would be at the top of the pyramid, and Mr. MacDonald and Mr. Lawrence would be at the next level of the pyramid. Presumably if these three can agree, something gets done. But the subjects on which these three can agree are exceedingly limited. They can agree that certain types of business-oriented renewal are desirable. They can agree that a certain highway or a parking plan is desirable. On the other hand, there are a vastly larger number of subjects which this group presumably would not only *not* agree upon, but which they would not even undertake to discuss: wages and steel prices being a case in point.

In Philadelphia, no fifty or a hundred people would agree on some of the matters that might be effectively treated by a much smaller group in Pittsburgh, and I suspect that Philadelphia is more typical of the rest of the United States than is Pittsburgh or Atlanta. Certainly none of the recent case studies suggests a pyramidal form of institution making decisions on a very broad range of issues such as that which Hunter has described.

Metropolitan decisions are a special case. Here the network of institutional connections and the flow of communication between power and influence constellations are weak, tenuous, or nonexistent. Suburban constellations of influence and power are typically unrelated or very remotely related to those which prevail in central cities. This is true whether we are discussing political machines or business groups. It is even more true when we deal with civic groups. The machinery for communicating needs, the machinery for assembling coalitions of interest, the machinery for reaching accommodation, scarcely exists. It is for this reason, it seems to me, that we have failed to mount metropolitan policies even where some have been proposed. The only instrumentalities for resolving such problems are governmental instrumentalities at the state or federal levels, and these are comparatively weak in their knowledge of, or ability and resources for negotiation with, the multiplicity of constellations of power which dominate the local affected areas. Why is anybody interested in the metropolitan area as a whole anyway? Any reasonably sober answer to this question, it seems to me, can lead only to the conclusion that nobody is interested. Nobody who has power and influence, nobody who has a stake in changing the flow of current processes, nobody who has resources to alter that flow.

III. TO IMPROVE RATIONALITY AND CONCENSUS

Guiding the Fact Component

If what has been summarized here, at too great length, is a reasonably accurate description of the actors and the actions involved, what are the implications of these structures and these processes for the future of urban growth?

First, we are dealing with a mixed system of public and private decision-making, influenced by market and nonmarket forces, and these interpenetrate at almost every point. The system is an open one. Many subjects are not the concern of existing organizations or interests. Many subjects are neglected. The system is a loose one. It is dependent upon both informal and formal connections, flows of communication in which there are gaps, varying degrees of awareness of problems or even of self-interest. In short, the system is characterized by opportunities for leadership and for change. The system has its expression in organization and institutions, in processes—ways of doing public and private business—and in policies, the residual of settled controversies. Any attempt to change the system which neglects any one of these areas is likely to prove inadequate for the intended purpose.

The dominant forces and the major decisions in metropolitan growth are market forces and market decisions. The constraints on market decisions are definable and in some degree measurable. It is characteristic of the market that it often operates without adequate facts or with incorrect facts. Frequently when the market decision-makers believe that they are operating on a basis of fact, inaccuracies or misunderstanding of the fact may be as important as the facts available. Market decisions are influenced also not merely by direct public policy decisions but also very heavily by the accumulated body of past decisions. Thus the property tax, the corporate income tax, the capital gains tax, prevailing standards of schools or highways—matters not in controversy at the moment in the arena of public policy—may be important determinants of market behavior. Any approach which would alter the consequences of market behavior as they have operated in recent years in urban and metropolitan development should carefully scrutinize this accumulated body of settled policy.

Nonmarket forces include the very powerful influences to which I have just made reference—the accumulated body of settled public policy. Nonmarket decisions are reached through a complex of public and private agents, through a network of communication, accommodation, and agreement which is always open to change if sufficient influence can be mobilized, if facts can be presented, if choices can be made clear, and the consequences of choices for particular interest groups can be brought home to those groups. The process of mobilizing interests, of forming coalitions of common interests, of establishing communications and liaison among them so that they are reading the same facts in the same way, is intricate but one in which there are great opportunities for leadership and great outlooks for change. The subjects of nonmarket decisions are often particular decisions within the framework of broader accepted policies, and while our institutions for decision-making, particularly the political ones, tend to be rather weak, there are unexplored opportunities for strengthening these mechanisms. These include particularly the role of the professions and the role of higher levels of government in the decision process.

Next, we should examine the fact basis for decisions regarding urban development. As has been indicated earlier, the market facts are not widely available or widely understood, yet this is the determining factor in an overwhelming majority of decisions being made. The simple act of providing the facts regarding market trends in usable form, accessible to deciders, would make a real difference in our urban development patterns and conceivably in urban development rates. In this connection it is to be noted that the importance of market facts is being increasingly recognized by business firms and that there is an apparent ground swell favoring the establishment of metropolitan market-data services which would provide common factual grounds for many kinds of business and public decisions. Since these facts are essential for transportation, land use, and housing planning purposes, it seems niggardly if we do not arrange the institutions through which they can be collected on a common basis, promptly processed in usable forms, and made available to all deciders. Indeed, the establishment of metropolitan-area data services is one of the most important leverage points in the evolution of metropolitan policies. I scarcely need point out that to have public agencies and private agencies operating from the same factual base would in itself provide much ground for getting rid of differences in perspective which so often prevail today.

Finally, there is the area of common assumptions regarding the meaning of the facts, common assumptions regarding the trends which are operative in the metropolitan area. These are not as readily handled as the fact problems, for they involve projections and forecasts. On the other hand, the range of interpretation of the trends is now probably much wider than it needs to be. If this range of interpretation could be appreciably narrowed, it might well be that we would find many participants in a development process operating in harmony as a result of their common understandings. Thus, bankers generally agree that the residential areas surrounding central business districts are declining and will continue to decline. In fact these areas have a use, the rates of change in them are ascertainable. In the light of these rates of change certain kinds of investments in them are probably sound. If there were a common understanding regarding these facts and what they meant with respect to the next decade or the decade thereafter, banker behavior might be radically altered.

Similarly, many people believe that our central cities are soon to be overwhelmingly populated by minority groups. I find this belief as firm in Washington, where minority groups now comprise more than half the population, as it is in another major metropolitan area where minority groups comprise less than 5 per cent. Obviously, these two cities are in exceedingly different postures, and the same inferences cannot possibly be drawn from the two very different sets of circumstances. Nevertheless, people behave as if these were similar situations. If we were able to forecast, for the residents of the second city, the rates at which their nonwhite population might grow and the economic consequences of those changes, and if such forecasts were accepted as realistic, the behavior in this city would probably be much less irrational than it is now.

The metropolitan development plan has an important role to play in achieving common consensus regarding the processes at work and the meaning of those processes for business, for people, for transportation, for social services, for all aspects of urban life. Rightly or wrongly, most of the actors in the situation tend to believe that there is some truth, some certainty, in a publicly announced and widely published plan. If we had better plans, which exposed their factual background, the reasons for the forecasts, and the reasons for the recommendations, and if we had plans which demonstrated with reasonable clarity that the plan was in fact attainable, such plans could have an enormously valuable unifying effect upon the behavior of autonomous actors in the development decision process. At least there would be a common understanding of what is actually happening and a common point of departure for analysis of what should happen.

Lastly, we come to the role of higher levels of government in metropolitan development decisions. Like the market and the local decision process, higher levels of government are pursuing segmental, separate, and often conflicting ends through policies whose actual effects are very rarely scrutinized systematically. If there could be agreement among these bureaucracies regarding, first, the facts; second, the trends with which policy must deal; and third, the standards which ought to be operative, these fact, trend, and standard signals would be rapidly communicated to the public and private agents of development at the local level. The number of cases of friction and controversy would be reduced. The opportunities for prompt public decision-making in accordance with agreed standards would be enhanced. And the frequency with which local officials would defer to the technical and policy judgments of higher levels of government would be considerably increased. This would relieve pressure on local officials where they are least able to take it—at the expense of transferring a larger share of the responsibility for development decisions to technicians and bureaucrats.

There are dangers in this of which I am fully aware. Nevertheless, I would suggest that some combination of metropolitan data service, a locally developed metropolitan master plan, stronger professional and community leadership, federal coordination, and improved technical standards for the several professions which are deeply engaged in development, form the basis upon which we will build a metropolitan development policy.

Guiding the Standard Component

The professions and bureaucracies exercise key functions in the decision chain. Professionals appear to be highly favored as communication links, information links and "bridge-men" between public and private institutions and, within private or public networks of power and influence, between the sub-constellations thereof. This peculiar role of the professions is illustrated in numerous case studies where an individual professional is entrusted with the liaison or communication role or performs that function on his own initiative. A business group which has no regular communication links with a competing business group retains a firm of attorneys. The attorney firm contains a member who knows the attorneys serving the competing business group. The two attorneys exchange information regarding their respective clients' policies or problems and discover that the two competitors are operating on a basis of different facts or on the basis of erroneous assumptions regarding the behavior of the competing group. The professionals make it their business to inform their principals that their facts may be suspect or that their assumptions regarding the behavior of their competitors may be wrong. The principals in turn check their facts or check with their competitors and realign their behavior in accordance with more realistic information or understanding. The same function operates widely among civic groups and among political organizations. Planners are in as peculiarly advantageous a position to perform these functions as are attorneys and bankers.

At another level we must recognize that many of the judgments, upon the basis of which principals make their decisions, are supplied by lower level professionals within their own organizations. These people, too, have connections with their counterparts in other organizations. They exchange information; they develop common understandings of what the facts are, or what a reasonable interpretation of the trends might be, or of what accords with their professional ideas of the desirable or the possible.

Further, the professionals have standards of behavior, standards of professional practice or procedures, which are a unifying element in the whole chain of decision-making. To the extent that these standards are well grounded and are commonly accepted by the professions, they provide a basis for doing business, for the exchange of information, for understandings which will lead successfully to action. Thus, the civil engineer in a municipal highway department utilizes standards of geometric design or standards of capacities for certain types of facilities which he knows will be acceptable to the district office of the state highway department and to the district engineer of the U.S. Bureau of Public Roads. And the landscape architect retained by a developer utilizes standards which he knows to be common to those of the FHA district office and the local subdivision control office in a suburban community. The re-examination or reformulation of these standards, a slow and protracted process, is nevertheless a foundation stone for more efficiently functioning urban growth patterns.

Bureaucracies also have their standards of behavior, their influences and guides, which, if consciously recognized, can become an agent of change. Poor old FHA is blamed for all sorts of inadequacies which are perfectly understandable from the standpoint of the chief underwriter in an FHA office. He is under instructions to insure bad loans, in dubious areas, without adequate criteria for selecting the risks which he will assume as opposed to those which he will not assume under these adverse circumstances. He knows all too well that in the past when similar bad risks have been undertaken, his organization has suffered loss of prestige or influence and some of his colleagues may have lost their jobs. It is understandable that he, as an individual, as a professional, and as a loyal member of an institution, should resist pressures to make what he regards as ill-conceived or inadequately analyzed decisions until it is very clear to him what the standards may be and that this type of policy has become effective public policy for which he and his organization will not suffer.

If we were to try consciously to realign the customary behavior of the professional and bureaucratic actors in metropolitan development, we could exercise considerable influence on the course of events. Again, fact and trend analysis would be useful, and a master plan would help. Beyond that, why not try directly to train these professions for new standards to meet new conditions?

Some Conclusions

It has been suggested here that new investment decisions affecting metropolitan growth are deeply influenced by market forces, the size and character of the public or private investors, interdependence of decision processes, professional standards, bureaucratic procedures, settled public policies and customary relationships. The direct exercise of public policy upon such decisions to shape metropolitan growth appears unlikely to be effective, not only because of the absence of metropolitan agencies of government, but also because of the inability of local governments to make decisions, the diffusion of public and private power and influence, and the indifference or divided interests of various publics.

Under these circumstances the most powerful guiding forces available may be the provision of comprehensive and systematic market data for the use of both private and public investment decision-makers. The development of metropolitan master plans, including the projections incident to them, would also tend to concert action into coordinated channels. Finally, the guidance of professional and bureaucratic standards of practice, through research and education, offers a potentially significant means for utilizing existing processes of communication and decision to secure collaborative action by public and private investors.

Each of these approaches is susceptible of implementation without serious challenge to existing institutions or the necessity for radical reorganizations. It should be possible to establish metropolitan-area data centers, to serve both public and private data needs, in each metropolitan area. Federal data-collecting agencies, local and metropolitan planning agencies, and private business would benefit from such a service and should support its establishment. There is increasing recognition, for instance, of the need for fairly elaborate data services on a continuing basis for transportation and land-use planning. Most of these data have significant private uses in market analysis and forecasting. If a data center is in existence, its use for the preparation of forecasts of population distribution, employment and income, public and private investments, and other indicators of change will follow as a service to governments and business.

The establishment of a metropolitan planning agency and the development of a metropolitan plan involve greater difficulties, though not insuperable ones. Quasi-official or private agencies of this type now exist in many metropolitan areas, serving as a means for reaching consensus on fact and trends and for setting goals which are observed, if not literally followed, by action agencies. Trend estimation and goal setting by community leaders, or technicians, or public agencies affect the course of action directly or indirectly. In some sense they become self-fulfilling prophecies, especially if they are used as guides by private investors, who suspect that the forecasts may be correct or the goals reflective of public policy, and by higher levels of government which make grants for public works.

Given these relatively noncontroversial functions, the technicians and the professionals have a basis for consensual, if not concerted, action. As the agents who negotiate and decide upon all of the little decisions, and many of the big ones, they have the power to secure very widespread compliance. A few big issues must be fought out, as periodic tests of the balance of power, or to secure distributive justice as among contending groups. But even here, most contests can be solved "by the experts" before they become contests, and the controversies can be focused on the real major policy issues. Recognition of the common stake in growth can often overcome competitive concerns about shares in the profit, especially where skilled agents are reasonably well informed on the facts, costs and benefits, and the balance of power.

NOTES

[1] He has written extensively on this matter. See, for example, James Bryant Conant, *Slums and Suburbs: A Commentary on Schools in Metropolitan Areas* (New York: McGraw-Hill Book Co., 1961).

[2] Floyd Hunter, *Community Power Structure* (Chapel Hill: University of North Carolina Press, 1953).

[3] Karl W. Deutsch, *Political Community at the International Level* (New York: Doubleday & Co., 1954), p. 57.

[4] Robert A. Dahl, *Who Governs?* (New Haven: Yale University Press, 1961); Charles R. Adrian, *Governing Urban America* (New York: McGraw-Hill Book Co., 1961); Morris Janowitz, *The Community Press in an Urban Setting* (Glencoe, Ill.: The Free Press, 1952); Edward Banfield, *Political Influence* (New York: The Free Press of Glencoe, 1961); Wallace S. Sayre and Herbert Kaufman, *Governing New York City* (New York: Russell Sage Foundation, 1960); Robert Wood, *Suburbia: Its People and the Politics* (Boston: Houghton Mifflin Co., 1958).

[5] James Burnham, *The Managerial Revolution* (New York: The John Day Co., 1941).

The Tactical Plan

Albert Z. Guttenberg

A question as old as human society itself is how to deal with the apparent contradiction between the private good of the individual and the good of society as a whole. Political thinkers have answered the question in many different ways, some by denying that the conflict has any real basis. For certain philosophers only the society and its agent, the state, are real and, therefore, any sense of a purely private good is illusory, an aberration to be suppressed or ignored. On the other side there are those who argue that individuals and their interests alone are real and that "society" is merely a convenient abstraction.

The mainstream of Western political thought, however, has always recognized both a private person and a public or corporate person; and though the respect given to their different claims or interests may change with time and place, the distinction itself is never wholly lost.

These two "persons" are endowed with legal rights in which their relationship to each other is defined and regulated. To anyone concerned with questions of urban form their legal relationship is a matter of considerable interest because it determines how public objectives are to be implemented and this, in turn, affects a number of other concrete societal relationships, including spatial relationships.

In a socialist system, where the public power is large, the method of implementation is one of direct enforcement. But where, as under conditions of democratic capitalism, the major decisions determining the course of events are for the most part in private hands, the situation is quite different. Here, any idea of enforcement is often out of the question. In this case, government becomes a problem centering on the question: how can private energies be *led* to contribute to a public objective? One aspect of our own political history has been a search for effective inducements.

Essentially, there are only two ways of securing the co-operation of private individuals when more direct controls are lacking—*persuasion* and *tactics*. Persuasion works on the motive of the individual so as to confirm it in the public point of view. By education and argument he is made to see that in the long run self-interest is better served when private action encompasses the public good. The argument is reinforced by holding up vivid images of the objective meant to move the observer by their very attractiveness.

But, while persuasion is useful for winning inner assent to the objective, it doesn't necessarily bring about a corresponding change in behavior. Accordingly, persuasion comes to be supplemented by more effective, if less direct, measures—by tactics.

The essential method of tactics is not to divert the individual from his pursuit of self-interest, but rather to change the field in which he acts, so that his private actions are more likely to follow paths which contribute to the realization of the public objective. Thus, to give a familiar example, a government wishing to encourage charitable activities may exempt income donated to those activities from taxation. Or, to give another example closer to our own interests, a city wishing to encourage the use of a certain transit line may lower the fares, improve the service, or avoid building a competing expressway. Perhaps all three. In none of these cases are individuals coerced, nor are they exhorted, but the environment which conditions their behavior is changed, and so it is hoped that their behavior may be altered in a way that favors the public purpose.[1]

With tactics, then, the purpose is not to win the assent of the individual. Assent was given when he or his representatives ratified the objective and made of it a goal for himself and others to follow.[2] Tactics are used to overcome the self-contradiction involved when the individual acts publicly and when he acts privately.

American society is one in which the larger part of social and economic initiative is still legally vested in private hands. Our purpose in this exploratory essay is to trace some of the effects of this basic feature of our national political constitution into a field where they have never yet been described in a systematic fashion—city planning.[3] Especially, in keeping with the general theme of this book, we wish to observe its effects on the notion of urban form. Persuasion and tactics as two different methods of influencing the behavior of private individuals become the bases of two different types of community development plan, a "goal plan" and a "tactical plan," with the result that urban form is made to appear under a double aspect—as an end state to be striven for, and as a means of achieving that end state.

As an illustration I have chosen the case of a hypothetical central city under conditions of metropolitan growth. Although the use of tactical planning is by no means limited to a situation of this type, I thought it desirable not to divorce the concept of tactical planning from an account of the situation in which it usually arises and finds its most dramatic expression. In the crisis of growth a particular objective often comes to predominate in the tactical planning of the central city. Our first concern here will be with the origin and nature of this objective.

I. FUNCTIONAL CENTRALITY AS AN OBJECTIVE

Ordinarily, a city is viewed in either of two ways—as a *society of people* seeking opportunities, in which case the industrial establishment appears as a place to work (or to shop, or to play),[4] and its location is judged to be good or bad with reference to the convenience of the worker; or as a *society of industries,* also seeking opportunities according to their own functional requirements. In this case people are still in the picture but their value is changed. They appear as localized factors of production (labor supply) along with other factors, or as the ultimate consumers of the industrial product (market). Their human aspirations matter only insofar as these affect their availability or their propensity to consume.

The essential difference between the two societies is this: In one case people are the subjects and industrial establishments the objects, while in the other case the reverse is true—industrial establishments are the subjects and people are objects. Each type of subject is faced with more or less immobility on the part of its object which stems from the latter's proper needs, and each tries to use the other, i.e., locate the other to its own advantage. In the total city, then, we see the struggle of two formative principles or interests, which though opposed, are also indissolubly joined, inasmuch as they make use of the same human and material elements—two spirits in the same body, as it were.

How do the human and industrial subjects, implying as they do different spatial orders, manage to come into contact in a way in which the requirements of both are generally satisfied?[5] The question goes to the heart of the problem of urban form, but it is not the direct concern of this essay. Here, in addition to what is stated in footnote 5, we can only note the obvious fact that neither subject is able to ignore the other's interest altogether. For if a community were organized solely from the standpoint of human convenience, its industrial capacity would suffer. On the other hand, a community organized strictly in the interest of industrial convenience or efficiency would finally injure or alienate its human base. Urban structure, therefore, is necessarily a compromise, a relationship of persons and facilities in which the human and industrial subjects are both served but neither of them optimally. In short, the total system has its own optimum. This fact rules out the possibility of either human or industrial convenience as a sufficient objective for urban planning.

The *political* city, as represented by a boundary line, is merely a part of the total arena in which the two subjects meet and work out a relationship to each other. But when, as a result of metropolitan growth, it becomes evident that this meeting can take place equally well under a variety of spatial forms (Figure 1),[6] not all of them favorable to the

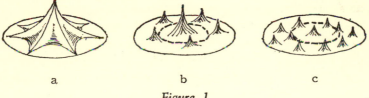

a   b   c

Figure 1

interests of the political *community*, then the latter becomes a third subject opposed to the unlimited subjectivity of both people and industry, i.e., it regards them both as objects to be used for its own purpose. By political community I mean here the inhabitants of the political city, such as the one represented in Figure 1 by the dotted line, who have in common a more permanent interest in the value of its territory.

The political community is impelled to influence metropolitan developmental forces in a direction which would increase that value. In other words, it seeks to retain or increase the economic or functional centrality of its territory in the region, although the objective need not take the crude form implied in Figure 1a.[7] More qualitative kinds of centrality may be sought.[8]

In its endeavor to bring about a distribution of metropolitan activities favorable to itself, the political community is hindered by the fact that its control over the behavior of the inhabitants of its own territory is limited, while beyond the boundary it has no control at all. Under these conditions, it has to resort to indirect or tactical measures, a requirement as urgent in the case of physical planning as it is in other forms of public action. In the following sections I have tried, first, to explain the general nature of tactical city planning, by comparing it with types of nontactical planning, and then to show how its use in a situation of metropolitan growth can lead to an over-all locational pattern in which the elements of urban form are made to subserve the objective of a political community.

II. TACTICAL PLANNING

The Goal Plan and the Tactical Plan

As subject, a polity begins to influence regional events in its own favor by projecting and publicizing an image of its objective. This image is represented by what I have called the goal plan. The goal plan, which may be spelled out in considerable land-use detail, is an optative statement of the size and form of the political city for the future year X. Typically, it shows the political city gaining or retaining a position of dominance in the region. To be sure, the image is credible, it bears some relation to existing opportunities in the region, but apart from its ability to persuade, to move people by its attractiveness, it includes no explicit measures for ensuring that these opportunities will be realized.[9] Therefore, in addition to the goal plan, another kind of plan is also required, one whose special purpose is to prevent the objective from being left behind by events over which the political community has only limited control, events largely determined by the innumerable decisions of private individuals, in other words by market forces. This is the tactical plan.

The Tactical Plan and Conventional Capital Programming

The tactical plan must, at least to begin with, bear a demonstrable relationship to the goal plan because of the fact that the latter is a known and publicized document, and any deviation from it has to be justified. The tactical plan may begin as a statement of the *order* in which the different elements of the goal plan should be undertaken. In this respect, tactical planning would appear to be identical with ordinary capital programming, but this is not the case inasmuch as capital programming, as it is usually practiced, and tactical planning are dealing with different problems and are guided by different considerations.

The problem of conventional programming is this: Given the goal plan for the year X to be realized over a period of, say, twenty-five years, what part should be carried out in the year X minus 24, what part in the year X minus 23, etc.? Here the guiding criteria, insofar as they are rational, are usually based on existing needs and trends. For example, highway A is prior to highway B because the present traffic pattern indicates a greater demand for A; or A is prior to B because present land-use trends indicate it will come into fuller use sooner.

This is quite different from the problem and procedure of tactical planning, which may be stated as follows: Given the goal plan for the year X, what steps should be taken first, not to anticipate present trends, but to *control* them—this to keep the plan from being made rapidly obsolete by a dynamic, changing environment?

Conventional programming, then, is concerned with carrying out the various elements of the plan, subject only to considerations of present or anticipated need, whereas tactical planning addresses itself to shaping actively the background conditions required by the plan, i.e., those general market orientations and locational preferences of the metropolitan community which are consistent with the features of the goal plan and necessary for its realization.

For example, if, according to a central city's goal plan, the city's central business district is to continue to be pre-eminent in the metropolitan region, then the continuing patronage of the regional population is a condition required for the realization of this feature of the goal plan. The tactical plan would then specify what is to be done first in order to increase the chances that this patronage does in fact continue uninterrupted, on the grounds that patronage once lost is not easily regained. Perhaps it will schedule improvements to the radial highways serving this center before improvements to highways serving other less important centers, even though improvements to all major highways are called for by the goal plan. In this case, highway B is given priority over highway A because it would facilitate trips in the direction of a preferred center and thus help to fulfill a major feature of the goal plan. And it would be given priority despite the fact that, as compared with highway A, it may satisfy a smaller number of present or (according to present trends) anticipated total trip requirements. From this example, it will be evident that there can be a conflict between conventional programming and tactical planning, i.e., between needs and goals as a basis for allocating community resources, between the community's present and its planned future.

In addition to prescribing the order in which the different elements of the goal plan should be undertaken, the tactical plan may also call for certain elements not appearing in the goal plan at all. Such elements represent modifications of the objective in the direction of greater realism. They tacitly recognize that in some areas conditions have already changed adversely to the goal plan beyond any possibility of reversal. But they are no less tactical as their purpose is to prevent conditions from changing even more adversely. Examples of this kind of modification of the objective will be given in the next section. At this point, we only wish to note that corresponding to the tactical plan, there is a spatial form—a configuration of elements comprising those parts of the total goal plan which are given priority or emphasized for tactical reasons, plus certain modifications of the goal plan.

III. TACTICAL FORM—AN EXAMPLE

The point has been stressed that to promulgate a plan is easy enough, but to put it into effect is not so direct nor simple a matter as utopian planning literature has commonly supposed. The main difficulty is in trying to keep market forces from behaving unfavorably to the plan, a requirement which often leads to results different from what was intended or hoped for. This fact will now be illustrated more concretely.

Regional Growth and Its Consequences

Among the events which change orientations and locational preferences is regional growth itself, by which I mean here the gradual adjustment of the regional structure to a larger territorial scale, the relocation of major facilities to serve a human and industrial population capable of wider dispersal.[10]

The process of adjustment involves the fortunes of individuals as well as of whole subcommunities of the region. Structural adjustments affect individuals by changing the positions of their homes or workplaces relative to the great activity centers of the community. The central political community is affected when, as a result of adjustments to larger scale, its territorial boundaries no longer include the total functional community of the region. Figure 2a illustrates one common

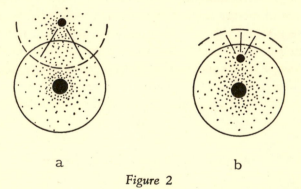

a   b

Figure 2

effect of growth: a service vacuum caused by excessive distance of population from existing centers comes to be filled by new centers outside the central city. The influence of the newer centers ranges deep into the service areas of the old, bringing about the reorientation of large numbers of people. It will be evident that the newer centers could just as well arise within the boundaries of the central city, as illustrated in Figure 2b. From the regional point of view either development would be acceptable, inasmuch as the difference between them may be a matter of only a few hundred yards. But to the political subcommunities of the region vying with each other for ratables, it may appear as a major difference in location.

The forces of metropolitan growth and change, then, include the following three factors: 1) technological advances, mainly in the field of transportation, which make possible the organization of regional life on a vastly wider geographical scale than has hitherto existed; 2) the numberless private decisions to relocate made in response to the expanding regional framework; 3) the conscious maneuvers of the politically independent suburb to bring about a shift of wealth and power in its own favor. For this is a common objective, even though it may be stated in far more ingenuous terms as a "workable tax economy" to be achieved by means of "limited and balanced growth." The land-use meaning of limited growth is large lot zoning and low density, the social meaning is exclusion of the poor and underprivileged, the fiscal meaning is low service costs. Balanced growth, on the other hand, means the selection of "choice," i.e., "non-child-producing" ratables, as well as the selection of the skilled and relatively well-to-do. The effect is to make of the boundary a line separating the costs from the benefits of regional growth.

The question naturally arises as to what corrective measures the central city can take in the face of this problem. The more direct measures are beyond the power of the city to impose: for example, the elimination of regional tax disparities, the enforcement of fair housing practices, any unusual restriction of the right of the individual to buy, sell, or locate where he chooses. Consequently, less direct measures have to be considered. To the planner, the question may appear as a problem in physical form. How can key regional facilities be arranged and programmed so as to bring about a pattern of private locational preferences and orientations more favorable to the central city, more favorable to the goal plan? This is but a specification of the more general question: how can self-satisfying private decisions be led to contribute to a public objective? The question, when it appears, marks a definite change in perspective: over-all community form has come to acquire a tactical meaning in addition to its ideal meaning as a right relationship between people and facilities.

The Tactical Variant

The diagrams in Figure 3 illustrate, in the broadest possible terms, the effect of tactical thought on a central city plan and, through the plan, on the form of the city.

Figure 3a, a hypothetical goal plan in schematic form, is an optative statement about the year X and after, a symbol of central city dominance in the region. Areas are to be served by radials, which relate them to the regional center, and by interstitial subordinate centers.[11] The purpose of the goal plan is more to state a desired objective persuasively than to plot a course of action for the intervening years.

The tactical variant of the goal plan (Figure 3b), on the other hand, is an action plan for the years prior to X and specifies the urgent measures to be undertaken in that period if the city is to retain its dominance. Its objective is to brake the centrifugal tendencies of money and population, in short, to keep the background conditions assumed by the goal plan from changing completely. Therefore, the elements of form become tactical elements: Peripheral substitute centers[12] (such as A) are contemplated, not so much to meet demand as to determine the place at which it will be satisfied—to compete with the substitute centers (such as B) beyond the boundary, or, sometimes (as in the case of C), to forestall the imminent development of a suburban center. As an alternative countermeasure, further development of city areas tributary to a suburban center (hatched) may be given a low priority, as compared with other areas of the city, in order to deprive the

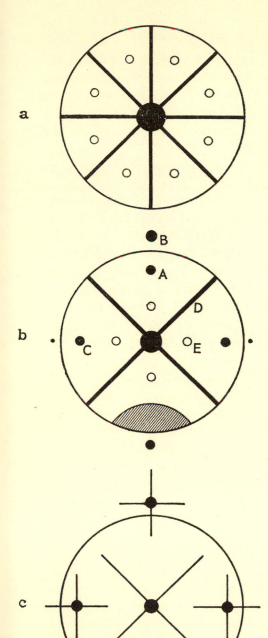

a   The Goal Plan

b   The Tactical Variant

c

Figure 3

suburban center of a market. Those radials of the goal plan (such as D) are emphasized which by-pass the suburban centers and which would establish the dominance of the regional center over a wider area. Radials feeding suburban centers may be downgraded in design, postponed, or altogether eliminated from the plan.

Tactical form is likely to result in yet other changes to the goal plan. For example, in Figure 3b (compare with Figure 3a), the regional center itself has undergone a reduction in planned size in favor of the substitute centers within the city or, to state the effect in terms of time, its improvement has been deferred. Also, the location proposed for subordinate centers (such as E) may change. However, these are the results of secondary adjustments; Figure 3b shows tactical form to be primarily a combination of certain elements of the goal form such as the by-passing radials, which are given priority for tactical reasons, and special tactical elements, such as the peripheral substitute city centers, which the goal form doesn't include. It represents a compromise between the two regional alternatives stated in Figures 3a, the goal form, and 3c, presumably the form which unopposed market forces and the action of neighboring communities would produce.

Perhaps it represents a stage of regional development intermediate between the present and future forms, likewise represented by Figures 3a and 3c.

IV. PERSPECTIVES

In the preceding section I have sought to make explicit an element present in the planning of large metropolitan areas, a tactical element which owes its motive in part to the political and fiscal disjointedness of an economic region.

Formerly, the major profit-generating functions were concentrated downtown. Now, changes in living patterns and technological advances have resulted in vast dislocations outward of people and economic activity. At the same time, the politically independent suburb has been able to select the more prosperous elements in this migratory wave, leaving the central city with a disproportionately large share of financial and social problems. Consequently, the city is impelled to take corrective measures even at the price of such departures from its stated physical development goals as may ensue from tactical planning—and this for the purpose of not entirely abandoning the objectives which those goals represent.

We will now carry our examination of this single instance of tactical planning somewhat further, to explore the meaning of certain metropolitan planning problems, and also to illustrate the problematic nature of tactical planning in general.

The Tactical Variant and the Private Interest

If, as has been done in the case of individual activities,[13] the uses of urban form are divided into two main types, city-serving and city-building, then the tactical variant of Figure 3b is an example of the latter type, for it represents the primacy of the city-building motives,[14] and only within the narrow limits they set are the city-serving functions of form to be carried out. This is a characteristic of any tactical plan, that it sets limits other than budgetary and legal limits to the service standards of the community. So doing, it implies that there is a more important objective than the *immediate* satisfaction of the individual person or industry who inhabits the city. In the case we have considered, the superordinate interest is the value of the common territory, which the tactical variant seeks to preserve. This viewpoint is consistent with the character of the political community as subject. But for the individual resident—person or industry—whose immediate interest is bound up with a particular site which he occupies, it may involve a cost, represented in Figure 3b by the planned shift of service from the center to the peripheral areas of the city. It may also involve a cost for the private resident outside the city, for if the tactical variant should succeed, it would curtail service beyond the boundary.

Is the cost justified? The answer depends on two factors; first, the intrinsic merit of the goal or objective in behalf of which a cost may be required. By the merit of the objective, I mean here its power, if achieved, to restore to the individual or to his descendants or successors more than was taken from him, or its power to save him from a greater future loss and this without depriving another individual. This is the ultimate moral test of any tactical plan.

The second factor is the aptness of the measures of the plan, their ability to achieve the desired objective. A single tactic, or a set of tactics, may be applied at the wrong place or at the wrong time, so that it fails. These failures do not invalidate the objective itself, but they are wasteful, and in this case the cost is not justified. This is the technical test of a tactical plan.

Here, however, we will concern ourselves only with the first criterion, the merit of the objective, as a test of the tactical variant of our example, and our viewpoint will be that of the total metropolitan community. In other words, we shall look at the plan as though it were a proposed metropolitan plan—this despite the fact that the plan was made by the central city for its own benefit. Cities, like individuals, act in their own interests, but this in no way alters the fact that at the same time they may be acting as the representatives of larger social forces. Metropolitan growth is not a wholehearted process. In certain respects, the tactical variant appears as an effort of the *total* metropolitan community, a concrete social, economic, and political organism, made up of the interlocking lives of multitudes, to preserve itself in the moment of growth, from the pain and cost of disruption which is one aspect of growth. These comments imply the existence of a fourth subject, the total metropolitan community, whose objective is the metropolitan optimum and from whose point of view the self-interested political communities of the region and their plans may appear as mere instruments, perhaps even as unwitting representatives. This is the light in which we now wish to regard the plan. In order to see it in this way, i.e., in order to avoid the prejudgment likely to be involved in knowing that the tactical variant is, in the first instance, the plan of a single political subcommunity of the region, it will be useful to view it momentarily in relation to a metropolitan problem of major importance—the urban renewal problem. From this point of view the plan will appear as one kind of plan which the metropolitan community may wish to regard as being in the long-term interest of the metropolitan resident, regardless of his location.

The Tactical Variant as an Urban Renewal Plan

As a special kind of planning interest, urban renewal is characterized by a concern with the older portions of a metropolitan region under conditions of growth, represented in Figure 3b by the area of the circle.

Metropolitan growth means a farther-flung population to be served, and as a result of the increased distances the older, central areas of the region are no longer entirely convenient places from which to serve them. Losing their normal time-distance relationships to a dispersing population, they become, as it were, dislocated.

Dislocated, the central areas undergo the ordeal of economic and social succession. Their original activities begin to leave them and are replaced by activities of another kind or quality. The process is a costly one with its accompaniment of personal, social, and environmental disorder—blight. As one of the major objectives of urban renewal is to eliminate blight or to prevent its occurrence, it follows that any plan to halt or retard the process of dislocation, or to limit its extent, is a kind of urban renewal plan.

It might be argued, then, that the tactical variant is an urban renewal plan since, in its case too, the purpose is to retard the dislocation of the older established areas of the metropolitan region. By inhibiting the rise of competing (i.e., substitute) activity centers at the periphery, the radius of regional development is shortened. As a result, the more central areas retain their usefulness as places from which to serve the regional population, and the establishments which use them for this purpose remain in their present locations, with all that this implies for a continuance of healthy economic life at the center. To be sure, the tactical measures, themselves, involve a planned shift of some activity outward, but presumably the shift is less extensive than what would take place if these measures were not applied (compare Figures 3b and 3c).

Considering the great strength of the forces of dispersal, and the weakness of the tactical measures considered here, the stabilization of present central activity is a doubtful undertaking, but not necessarily hopeless. Much depends on the extent to which existing sites are replaceable elsewhere in a region. A good harbor, for example, the base of many activities, cannot be easily replaced, nor can the qualities of site sacredness or historicity. In one case, value depends on physiography and in the other on absolute location. In the possession of rare or unique site qualities, cities differ greatly; but where they exist tactical planning would have powerful allies.

To be sure, we have considered only one aspect of regional

growth—the cost of disrupting the present pattern of development. But what of the benefits of reintegration at a larger scale? [15] From this point of view, the dislocation of the central city, which it is the purpose of the tactical variant to resist, may, in the long run, be a salutary development. This is especially the case when we consider that the metropolitan area as a whole is itself in competition with other metropolitan areas, and that a broader, more comfortable, and more efficient spatial setting may be required for its future economic welfare, including the welfare of the central city itself. Steps to hinder the process of dislocation, then, could well be considered retrograde.

Does the greater social waste lie in encouraging the disruption of the existing pattern, or in resisting this disruption? Or is the question itself a false one? Is it only through the mutual opposition of these two forces that the metropolitan optimum can be found, or can find itself? These are but different ways of asking if the tactical variant is justified, if it would finally compensate that metropolitan resident who may have to pay the price.

The Tactical Planner and the Public

American government is government for the people and so the people's values, insofar as they are not satisfied in the market place, become public objectives embodied in great programs of civic improvement. Other values, those that pertain to individual rights, come to government in a negative form, as restraints upon its actions. Thus, government is entrusted with broad responsibilities, but it is seldom given corresponding powers of effectuation. It is this disparity of governmental ends and means which is one of the distinguishing features of our society, some of whose effects we have sought to trace here. It has been shown that the very insufficiency of means calls forth a special response in the field of city planning, a tactical use of urban form. To be sure, we have limited ourselves to a single example, but in this example the essential phenomenon is contained. One is able to distinguish between the tactical method itself and a particular use to which it may be put.

Like persuasion, the basis of the goal plan, tactical methods represent, in the main, the efforts of a community of free men to take a conscious direction, or to resist a direction, i.e., not to drift, not to rely on the "unseen hand of the market" to produce a desired social result. But they go beyond persuasion in trying to overcome the frequent contradiction between public and private action.

As a response to an ancient problem of democracy, as a means of combining personal freedom with community planning, tactical methods show great promise. But the difficulties which stand in the way of this promise are also great. Not the least of these difficulties are the demands which tactical planning makes on the planner himself, who must use it as a technician, and on the public which must authorize its use. If they can be met, then urban communities may look forward to a new era of self-mastery.

For the planner, tactical planning requires a shift of focus from ends to means. With relatively few means at his disposal he is expected to produce large, transforming and, of course, predictable effects on community life. This presumes considerable knowledge of urban dynamics in general and of his own community in particular.

From his dalliance with long-range objectives, he is called upon to subject these objectives to the contradictions of time, by programming and putting into effect intermediate arrangements which contribute to the realization of these objectives at the same time that they differ from its popular symbol, the goal plan.

How are these differences to be presented to the public and

explained? Here we encounter what is perhaps the major nontechnical problem of tactical planning. For, while the goal is fully public and easy to grasp, the tactical means, being largely esoteric, pass out of public view into the hands of the expert, the planner. The criteria of the public as a critic of programming decisions are based on its observations of existing conditions and trends, on obvious needs, and on the dramatic features of the goal plan. Therefore, a purely tactical programming of the objectives, not necessarily meant to meet present needs, is likely to appear quite arbitrary and unreasonable. Here, it should be understood, it is not a question of winning the public's approval of the objective. This, presumably, has already been accomplished with the ratification of the goal plan. What is needed is public approval of the tactical means.

Can this approval be secured? The American public is likely to be impatient with the distance between the present fact and the future goal. It is hardly likely to endure the devious route to be followed in order to reach that goal. In submitting the tactical plan to the public, then, the planner is presenting the implications of a goal plan, and in so doing he is subjecting it to a test far more critical than if he merely presents the "bill" in terms of financial costs. In short, he is testing the seriousness and durability of the public purpose itself, for this is what the goal plan represents. As a result of this confrontation, the public may decide to rethink its objectives a little more carefully, perhaps a little more realistically. But if it retains its objectives, then it is better prepared to realize them because it is forearmed with knowledge of their implications in time. These considerations alone are enough to justify tactical thought and planning.

NOTES

[1] Strictly speaking, of course, persuasion is itself a kind of tactic, but here I would like to restrict that word to mean a change in the field of action rather than in the consciousness or motive of the private actor.

[2] This is only to say that an individual, in approving a goal, i.e., in giving open or tacit consent to it, implicitly approves of its implementation by indirect as well as by direct means. It does not imply that the legality or desirability of any specific tactic is beyond challenge, that an end justifies any and every means.

[3] However, see Martin Meyerson, "Building the Middle-Range Bridge for Comprehensive Planning," *Journal of the American Institute of Planners*, XXII (Spring, 1956), especially pp. 60-61. In this article Meyerson in effect calls for a "tactical plan."

[4] The term industrial establishment is used here most broadly to mean any establishment where a good or service is produced. In this sense even a playground or shop is an industrial establishment.

[5] The two fundamental moments of human life are work and rest (which includes the enjoyment of the fruits of work, i.e., re-creation). At work, man treats himself as an object, but at rest he reaffirms his subjectivity. This double relationship to self is the root of the difference between the human and industrial subjects.

The duality is reflected in the organization of both time and space. In time it takes various forms: workday and Sabbath, week and weekend, etc. The two states alternate: now the human subject prevails and now the industrial subject.

In space it takes the form of structural relationships. For an approach to the general features of the spatial or structural solution to the problem of duality see A. Guttenberg, "Urban Structure and Urban Growth," *Journal of the American Institute of Planners*, XXVI (May, 1960), especially p. 105.

[6] A. Guttenberg, *ibid.*, p. 109. In Figure 1, the conical mounds represent densities or concentrations of regional economic activity.

[7] In Figure 1a, as compared with 1b and 1c, the degree of regional economic and functional centrality possessed by the political city (enclosed by the dotted line) is greater and, presumably as a result, the value of its territory is higher.

[8] Compare Donald Foley's essay in this volume, "An Approach to Metropolitan Spatial Structure." Foley sees in contemporary metropolitan planning two different approaches, the "adaptive approach," which views the metropolitan community as process and seeks to influence developmental forces at work, and the "unitary approach," which aims for a single metropolitan form as a goal, the latter flowing "logically from the best traditions of architecture." Foley's distinction is a valid and useful one. However, it is apparent that there is a far more powerful force in the field than architecture contributing to the prominence of the "unitary" approach, namely, the territorial interest. Metropolitan form is a factor

to which a political community can hardly afford to be indifferent, because this is the factor which, perhaps more than any other, determines the locational value of its territory. Therefore, the political community, the author of the plan, is impelled to seek a preferred metropolitan form, one which maximizes the value of its territory. In practice, therefore, the two approaches are related to each other as are ends and means.

Even where metropolitan competition is not a factor, the "unitary approach" is required, for we have seen that one purpose of a plan is to persuade, and this means projecting a single, unambiguous image which will move private individuals in a desired direction.

[9] Most master plans are goal plans in this sense. In a recent illuminating article Robert B. Mitchell speaks of "wouldn't it be nice if—" plans which do not prescribe methods of attainment. See Robert B. Mitchell, "New Frontier in Metropolitan Planning," *Journal of the American Institute of Planners*, XXVII (August, 1961), 169-175.

[10] A. Guttenberg, *op. cit.*, pp. 107-108.

[11] A subordinate center is one of the two basic types of subcenter in the urban field. It corresponds to a lower level of community than the total region and, therefore, in the function it performs for the regional resident, complements rather than competes with the regional center.

[12] The second basic type of subcenter is the substitute center. The substitute center is "insubordinate" to the regional center whose functions it duplicates, or attempts to duplicate, for all or part of the region.

[13] Alexandersson, Gunnar, *The Industrial Structure of American Cities* (Lincoln: University of Nebraska Press, 1956), pp. 14-15.

[14] In the present context city-preserving would be a more appropriate term than city-building.

[15] While one objective of urban renewal is to prevent the occurrence and spread of blight, another is to give the total metropolitan community a broader and more comfortable spatial setting, one more in harmony with present day living patterns and technical capabilities. Both objectives are very much present in comtemporary urban renewal thought but, as our diagrams indicate, they are not necessarily compatible.

Summary:
Planning and Metropolitan Systems

John W. Dyckman

The metropolis is a system much described and little understood. We know that it has emerged at its present scale only in the last hundred years, and that this phenomenon appears as a phoenix-like birth from the ashes of the old city, which was a manageable and easily recognized political and social unit with fixed boundaries. By an accident of history, the metropolis has grown up in an era in which national states are mature and well consolidated, and are even in the process of forming supranational units. Students of the normative policy sciences have been engrossed in the study of the behavior and strategy of these larger units, and have neglected the constituent urban units. Economics and political science, in particular, have been preoccupied with the national state as the unit of analysis.

Sociology, which has been more descriptive and "positive" than its sister social sciences, despite its normative origins, has given greater attention to the city. Sociologists have described the distribution of all kinds of phenomena of contemporary society, from its pathology to its occupational division of labor, as correlates of urban space. The social ecologists of the 1920's, and generations of sociologists since, have found it convenient to plot social behavior along the convenient geographic scales of city maps. Fundamentally, of course, they have been interested in the social systems in which occupations and status, rewards and punishments, have been assigned, rather than in the operation of the space system. Still, this convenient overlap with the dimensions of geographic space and distance provides the physical analysis of the city with most of its clues for behavioral analysis. Taken with the administrative fortune that requires reporting of statistics by civil divisions, social ecology has furnished the raw material for much traditional metropolitan analysis.[1]

At first glance, the traditional ecological models appear to be ideal devices for describing and analyzing the city. Like many other models in the social sciences, they borrowed heavily from natural science. Early "social ecology" formulations of the city were based in part upon plant biology, with strong borrowing from evolutionary conceptions stressing the competition for sustenance and survival. The competitive tie permitted the theories of social ecology to mesh with theories of urban land economics which were developed from models of market competition. The apparent determinism of these views irked normative sociologists from the start.[2] Herbert Gans recently raised the objection that "ecological explanations of social life are most applicable if the subjects under study lack the ability to *make choices,* be they plants, animals, or human beings."[3]

In the market-ecology model, this is not strictly true, for the individual decision units do make choices; but the choosers are unable individually to affect the total outcome; and if they band together, the model must be changed. Gans's characterization also draws attention to the fact that the ecological model, as a competitive scheme, is most applicable in situations of extreme scarcity where all decisions tend to be marginal. Much of the important urban-shaping behavior in American society today, as Wheaton's essay in this book shows, is intramarginal, and not shaped by the pressures operating in the naturalistic models. But even if the competitive models were predictive of observed behavior, the city planners, like the normative sociologists and reformers with whom they share common origins, would want to change the outcome. To understand where to apply pressures to effect changes they would need different analytic conceptions of urban behavior.

Although ecology is not quite blind, its only guide is the classical "hidden hand." The more manipulative and interventionist arts require a closer look at the heavers and shovers. At the very least, change in the actions of men might be made by changing the information available to them at the time of decision to act. The normative study of subsystems or "micro" models in economics (e.g., the firm) and the extension of economic decision criteria to research strategies have helped to focus attention on the decision-maker. The ambitious "structural-functional" schemes of sociological theorists like Parsons attempt to provide an analytic framework for studying individual action in a social context. But the study of "decisions" as units of data is a "positive" first step in the ultimate normative analysis of an urban action system. The Wheaton paper shows how such analysis may be elicited from the descriptive measurement of decisions.

Systematic analysis of metropolitan decisions by social reformers or city planners or others seeking to make practical use of the analysis requires some severe simplification of the real world. A "system" of actors and actions which are important for the prospective action ends must be chosen from the very large number available. The system chosen must be fitted hierarchically into the other systems which are used by the analyst. The dissection of behavior poses great problems in the organization of knowledge; the pieces broken out this way must be picked up and put in a pattern. Several different metropolitan systems are chosen by the authors of these essays.

Conventional models abstract from reality in other ways as well. Most of the formal models of theory, physical or social, are *closed*. The systems are in equilibrium, usually shut off from upsetting shocks from outside the system. This assumption poses more difficulty for the policy model than for the analytical model, but the closed system—and even mechanistic thinking—has been a companion of much physical planning of cities. The ordinary land-use plan is one such system, as is any conventional accounting scheme.

Indeed, it might be argued that scientific analysis is impossible without closing the system which is being examined. We have not been able to devise intellectual constructs which can handle the open system and the task of doing so may be inherently hopeless. Any system which is exchanging influence with its environment is open, and all the phenomena of real life which we abstract for analysis are in the process of interacting with some environment. Hence, all are open. But an environment is usually taken for granted even in ordinary statements of fact, despite the necessity, which Churchman has pointed out, of making any assertion conditional on a particular environment.

Unfortunately for systematic urbanists, the environment for much of the abstraction of social science—sociological, economic, or psychological—is the metropolis. Nor does it help that a majority of scholars, like a majority of people in the world, lives in cities. There is, understandably, a sizable body of amateur and semiprofessional opinion about the state of urban life, and about the impact of the urban environment on behavior. Essays such as these could not, however, have been generated by an amateur interest. Rather, the writings in this book represent a highly professionalized concern with the ordering and systematic study of the modern metropolis and "post-civilization" urban forms. The writers are uneasy with the mechanical analogies of earlier systems and uncomfortable about the absence of symbolic processes, communication, and meaning in the more deterministic ecological models. For my part, I am almost equally uneasy about the academicism and abstraction of the Parsonian structures in some of the essays, but the task of treating social systems with power and generality while maintaining concreteness is an exceedingly formidable assignment.

The contributors to this volume are attempting to come to grips with the problems posed by planning for open systems whose course of development is the result of decisions made by many individuals exercising a wide latitude of choice. It may be that planning for such systems is doomed to defeat almost before it can start. Yet the challenge posed by these writers is worthy of a hearing. Traditional planning, which has focused on the master plan as a *product*, a discrete guide to a fixed form of future development, is undergoing substantial adaptation in the minds of planners themselves, as well as in the view of other governmental practitioners.

In part, this is a recognition of the greater complexity of urban growth and development, and in particular, of the considerations entering into individual decision. In part, it is a recognition of the claims of modified cultural relativism, which sees functional uses in activities not hitherto considered worthwhile, and which sees the dysfunctional character of many imposed solutions.

To some, these statements will add up to fundamental reservations about the efficacy of planning, or even the possibility of planning. This is certainly not the intent of the authors. But their contributions suggest that the business of planning is considerably more complex than has generally been recognized by planners. It would be clear from points emphasized again and again in these essays that the urban community is an extremely complex system, open to change in many directions. In practice it may be difficult to determine the number of significant variables which constitute the environment of this system. Only by developing techniques competent to deal with "organized complexity," to use Warren Weaver's term,[4] can planning hope to deal with a changing city as a manageable artifact. While many developments in data handling and data organization, the rise of computers, and great conceptual advances in scientific methodology all promise some hope for this task, it appears that little progress can be made until the existing underbrush of poor and weak definitions is cleared and pruned.

The essays in this volume are aimed at clarifying some of the key issues in the developing confusion of planning and urban studies. It is ironic, in a society which does not welcome public planning, that there should be so much support for planning that most difficult artifact of civilization, the city itself. Perhaps it is because the city so well dramatizes the potential gains from planning that the city planners have been encouraged in their undertaking. The paradox is that planning for cities is potentially palatable in our society, but the understanding of the city which would permit the planner to meet the main strictures of planning method is largely lacking. In short, the planner is given freedom to plan in an area where planning may be presently most difficult. To the critic (and these are, in large part, critical essays) who looks deeply at the nature of planning activity in the urban scene, there are three important questions for which answers are presently most unsatisfactory. These are as follows:

1. What is urban *space,* or the spatial aspect, of city and regional planning? Since planning has been tied to local government, the conceptions of urban systems employed by planners have followed closely the lines of political and governmental administration. It is true that planners have called attention to the functional unity of metropolitan systems as compared with central city and suburban entities

within the system, but the idea that the metropolis has a discrete space, a "turf" of its own, remains deeply rooted. American local government itself is strongly place-conscious.

But space, used in this context, tends to be geographically determined. It is fixed by measurement on the ground. The functionalist view which is ascendant in these essays finds this distinction of activity by place of occurrence exaggerated. Webber, in particular, attacks the "place base" of the typical city plan—and city-planning outlook. He extends the notion of functional interdependence to plead for new meaning for "community." The relevant communities for Webber are the communities of functional interest, which in our society he believes are increasingly transcending geographic limitations. He proposes tracing interdependence in a context of activity that goes well beyond the local community for at least a sizable portion of participants.

In this emphasis he has come closer to some of the functional anthropologists than to traditional city planning. He might point out that there are societies—the Tiv in Nigeria are a commonly cited example—of a culture which has no meaning for fixed territory or place, in the sense in which our geographers identify it and our culture in general uses it. He might also cite the studies in social psychology and perception, going back to Kurt Lewin and his psychological ecology, which contend that psychological space confronting the decision-maker can be identified and studied as a meaningful space system. But Webber need not go this far. He can simply point out, as he does, that executives, intellectuals, and officers of businesses and universities even now are members of communities which span enormous distances in geographical space. Margaret Mead made this point less systematically in a paper in the *Annals of the American Academy of Political and Social Science* a few years ago.[5]

The main point of the criticism raised by Webber in this

connection is that planning for a discrete and geographically self-contained space does not of itself constitute planning for an equally discrete and self-contained system of activities. But it is the activity, presumably, which creates the dynamics of change in the very geographical system for which traditional planning has been carried on. Historical boundaries—and geographic space in general—may be poor bases for the selection of elements to make up a meaningful system for analyzing metropolitan activities. That they persist as the chief criteria for inclusion in the conceptual systems of urban planners in America is testimony to (a) the *land* preoccupation of these planners, and (b) to the relatively low urgency of much of their work, which does not press upon them the importance of other systems.

2. The second important question to which these essays are addressed is to what extent the plan is a statement of a desired end-state, and to what extent it is a delineation of a process of change. The traditional land-use plan, with its fixed allocations of space and its neat compartmentalization of activities, appears unnecessarily static to these authors. In spirit, they are all approaching the ideal of developmental planning advocated by Robert B. Mitchell.[6]

The views of Webber on urban space, which are the boldest expression in the essays above, are the speculative extension of insights developed in the researches of Mitchell and Rapkin,[7] Rannells, and others on urban land uses. In Rannells's *Core of the City*,[8] for example, the view is expressed that the activities generated by the land use of a single plot cannot be understood from a consideration of the plot alone, but must be seen as a part of the system of urban activities linked by functional relations. Webber and Foley greatly extend the theoretical statement of this view.

But the implication of their work goes further. Conceptually, they are allied with those planners who hold that plans must be dynamic, dealing with processes of change over time, and with the whole process of development of the community. In the past, this has led some planners to stress programming, particularly capital budgeting and public-works scheduling. The position espoused by Mitchell, and endorsed implicitly by the authors in this volume, would extend the analysis to all major determining forces in city growth, private as well as public. Wheaton shows the interdependence between private and public decisions, effectively discrediting the dualism that has falsely polarized them. The question as to the programming of these forces is, of course, a political one. With the exception of Guttenberg's sidelong glance from his strategic perch, none of the essays deals with the last question, which is a well-worn issue from the economic debates of the 'thirties and early 'forties.

All these essays reflect some dissatisfaction at the unfilled gap between the long-range physical-plan view of the community on the one hand, and the narrowly space-bound project plan on the other. Meyerson's address to a national planning convention, several years ago, called attention to the need for bridging this gap.[9] Recently, the planning profession has become increasingly conscious of the need for developmental planning. In urban renewal, for example, the creation of the Community Renewal Program has been an attempt to answer just this need. But techniques for planning a complex evolving system remain relatively undeveloped.

All the essays in this volume, in one form or another, represent efforts to come to grips with this task of dealing with organized complexity. For the most part, they choose to do so at a first descriptive stage. Despite the fact that the authors are conscious of the nature of these processes, and at least one of them addresses himself directly to a tactical problem, there is much more work to be done on the tasks of identifying critical structural elements, phasing programs, strategic timing of interventions, managing several dimensions at a single moment, and breaking down complex processes into analytical stages.

The time dimension, in which ongoing processes of change are decomposed into individual static time-slices, is the arena in which the tactical skills need be sharpened. American city planning has polished its technique in the long-range goal plan and the short-range project plan, leaving the intermediate developmental planning untended. Wheaton, who here analyzes development decisions in such detail, has been a leader in pressing for comprehensive development planning in urban renewal. Largely through his efforts, the "programming" of development actions in the Community Renewal Program has become a requirement of federally aided programs. This is a promising step toward the "middle-range bridge" which Meyerson called for.

The gulf between the long-range planner and the development planner is, however, more than a matter of years. Long-range planners identify with a "humanistic" tradition of the seekers after ideal states. They are more concerned with where we are going than with how to get there, for they see as their task the reshaping of the image of the future in the present. Development planners, they feel, are bureaucrats preoccupied with means at the expense of ends.

For their part, the development-minded planners see the long-range plans as largely arbitrary creations doomed to gather dust on city shelves, or, at worst, insensitive visions liable to tangle the business of the city in growing confusion. They see the community as a complex web of behavior that cannot be summarily directed to a far-off goal, but one that must be managed and coaxed and led. Instead of painting and repainting the image of the future, these planners would have the profession focus on the more incremental improvements in efficiency and amenity, on patching up severe dislocations in urban functioning, and on encouraging the realization of present aims and aspirations of the community.

3. The identification of the goal—or goals—to which the strategy of city planning is directed forms the third major issue to which the authors of this volume turn. Both Webber and Foley have tied their insights into the complexity of the first and second issues (the meaning of urban space and the processes of urban growth) into a noose which they slip over the long-held planning simplification of the goal question. Foley attacks the naïve view of community which has characterized much city planning. In particular, he wishes to expose the weakness of what he calls the "corporate unity" simplification which underlies the goal statement of the master plan, and to oppose to it the view of functional interdependence and plurality of interest held by sociology and social anthropology. He is not explicit in indicating whether the resolution of the plural interest comes about by some process of bargaining, aided by "functional" compromises, or by some other mechanism.

Webber, in attacking the place base of the typical plan, and extending the notion of functional interdependence in his plea for new meanings for "community," traces interdependence in an activity context that goes well beyond the local community. Both Webber and Foley cast doubt on our ability to identify a clear-cut community interest short of having a successfully descriptive model of the community. That is, the implication of their position is that judgments of "functional" and "dysfunctional" contributions to community cannot be made without a highly explicit and detailed picture of the structure of the community.

Guttenberg, in turn, while conceding the existence of plural interests and the importance of functional interdependence, is concerned with the planning problem of dealing effectively with these realities, given the existence of an institutionalized planning interest. He proposes a tactical plan which can serve the long-run goal through a process of short-run adjustments. It is characteristic of utopian writers that they have nurtured the idea of a stable self-correcting social system which, once pushed in the right direction, would continue to run itself.[10] The critics of the naïve utopianism in planning see this system as open to all kinds of changes from outside. A strategy is needed to adapt to these exogenous forces impinging on the system. This strategy requires specification of the way in which the elements of the system adapt to and modify these forces.

In a provocative analogy, Norton Long has suggested that the urban community ought to be viewed as an ecology of games.[11] That is, the activities of the community might be divided into distinguishable contests, and the area presided over by these contestants, who are playing according to the prevailing rules in that sector, would constitute the most significant division of urban space. Presumably, too, different contestants would have their own appropriate strategies for each of the games. Wheaton's spheres of decision fit this formulation well.

Guttenberg talks about a strategy of one of these games for one contestant—the planning agency. At the same time, he seems to equate the strategy of the planning agency with the appropriate strategy for the community. That is, he accepts the institutional delegation, by some appropriate political procedure, of the contending interest of the community as "structure" to the planning agency, which is the interpreter of that structural interest.

Why have these authors, coming together in this volume, chosen to stress these points? First, and most obviously, it would be easy to say that they have all had training in social science rather than in design, and the obvious, certainly, is pertinent. But the concern of these writers goes beyond the obvious. The authors may be calling attention to the fact that contemporary city planning has lost sight of functional links between its utopian goals and the apparatus of enforcing its programs. In the sociological sense, a fair share of the machinery of city planning is "dysfunctional." The planners, behaving as any group which has undergone recent and thoroughgoing institutionalization, tend to seize upon bureaucratic instruments as the substance of their activity. Thus, zoning becomes an end in itself, and the presumptive gains from segregation of land uses and limitation on the character of use may disappear from sight. The authors would restore the perspective of city planning in this struggle to establish a more appropriate "functionalist" foundation.

City planning, which is implemented through land-use and public budget controls, affects many aspects of community life, but addresses itself in a particularly direct fashion to the public or semipublic "community facility." Its greatest impact falls on those community facilities requiring substantial physical development, e.g., parks, playgrounds, filtration plants. The importance of public investment in shaping the pattern of private land and building development is suggested by Wheaton. Its force is felt less directly in less space-bound programs, such as health and nursing, marriage counseling, aid to dependent children, etc. While space is a convenient "base" variable for measuring some sociological phenomena, as the ecologist long ago demonstrated, it is not satisfying to contemporary sociologists. For one thing, it imposes a single type of structure—the geographical—in an ascendant position as an explanatory variable. Many sociologists feel that spatial relations ought to be treated as dependent variables. Gans, for example, has argued persuasively for the more significant influence of class and other more clearly "sociological" variables in the determination of significant urban relationships.

The present volume is necessarily ambivalent on this issue. Though we speak of "community" as if it were a well-defined and easily recognizable entity, and though it is implied that "community facilities" are perfectly discrete subjects, they are nonetheless ambiguous notions. Planning cannot be purely naturalistic; it is bound close to notions of *purpose*. As a result, in efforts to frame analytic definitions of *community* the definitions cannot help but be colored by the goals that one seeks to analyze. It is difficult to define either "community" or "facility" without having reference to the *purpose* of people in congregating together or in framing institutions for providing the services, yet it is these very goals that planners typically propose to investigate.

This difficulty is well illustrated by consideration of the content of such "naturalistic" definitions as have been applied to urban society by the ecologist. An ecological definition of "community" as a functional, spatial-temporal order resulting from competitive, impersonal symbiotic relations between human animals also has its own teleology; in specifying the kind of interaction that makes a community, to the exclusion of other observable kinds of interaction (ascription or cooperation, for example) it establishes a kind of competitive equilibrium as a community "goal." The kind of consensus with which planning is chiefly concerned is then assigned to *society*, which is seen as a moral, rather than a natural, order.

There seems to be no advantage here in so limiting the notion of "community," or in distinguishing spatial-temporal "community" from the time-binding "society." Nor is it proposed to discuss the physical pattern of the "community" apart from social purposes. This means that the authors necessarily smuggle in some of their own concepts of community teleology; that is apparent in the Guttenberg treatment of strategy for communities in development policy.

The authors of these individual essays are not of one mind

on these questions. Guttenberg, for example, reminds us that "urban structure . . . is necessarily a compromise, a relationship of persons and facilities in which both subjects are served but neither of them optimally." Wheaton's data provide evidence for this view, though the purpose is to change the terms of exchange. Foley recommends that we first determine the nature of the functioning of the social system, and then design an appropriate physical environment as a base for that system. Webber at times seems to imply that the social system will find its own base, or pattern, of physical facilities.

Now, to the measure-bound scientist, the very definition of system requires control. Thus, the operations researcher, Martin Ernst,[12] in an excellent paper on systems analysis, defines a *system* as "a collection of functions and operations dominated by, and controlled for, a set of common objectives." Perhaps the persistently difficult element in coming to grips with the subjects treated by these writers is the difficulty of finding a set of common objectives for the contemporary urban community. As we have seen, Norton Long sees this as essentially a feckless enterprise. Instead, he would relegate the search for unitary objectives to a descriptive exercise cataloguing the various objectives of the players in a complex game. At times, both Webber and Foley lean to this view. But Guttenberg eschews it. He holds the more modest position. For him, planning is now a fact of contemporary life. What is more, the planner represents a responsibly delegated public interest. If nothing else, it is the interest of the city against the suburb. In such a capacity, the planner does well to protect that interest, and to seek a feasible ground for a minimum stand for the city.

For Guttenberg, political facts of life are ruling. The functionalist analysis of the sociologist which shows city and suburb as part of a single metropolitan social and economic system is bled of pertinence when compared with the life struggle of the municipality for self-determination and for a ground of rational policy which can be defensibly pursued toward a common welfare. The functional interdependencies of the metropolitan system are recognized by Guttenberg, but he does not accord them special significance. For him, the significant fact of life is the existence of a boundary between city and suburb. This boundary is admittedly *not* "functional," but it is nonetheless real for all that. The ultimate strategy for the city is to recognize these functional interdependencies and turn them to some tactical advantage for the core city. The tactical plan of Guttenberg is paradoxically one of accommodation; the functionalist cries of Webber and Foley and the decision analyses of Wheaton are essentially reconstructionist.

By focusing on *process,* all these authors have drawn attention to one of the weaknesses of traditional physical planning. The physical plans emphasize a desired future state, without a clear view of the processes by which that state is achieved. This emphasis is only natural. The preferences of human beings are for "states," not for processes—except in the unlikely instance of people who enjoy the game just for the playing. But as Bauer says, "His [read "the planner's"] very efforts to keep it [that is, a social system] alive will ensure its eventual transformation into something which will have to be called another 'system'. . . . All of the above is *not* to say that social control and social planning are impossible; but rather close control and planning are possible only on a relatively short-run basis with a continuing revision of objectives and methods according to the evolution of society, and the problems with which it is faced." [13]

The ideal planning operation would combine both interest in process and a desire for goals. It would be sufficiently utopian to stir men's vision and aspirations, and sufficiently skilled in analyzing the processes of effectuation of those ends and in organizing and deploying resources for their attainment to bring about the utopian state. No such ideal combination can be found anywhere in human affairs. The best we can hope for is steady improvement—a road that brings us ever closer to the new goals that are constantly being re-created out of the images of the old ones. For a variety of reasons, the authors in this volume see their contributions as therapeutic.

Too long a preoccupation with the static state has made the long-range physical planning of American communities insensitive to the processes of growth and change. Too close attention to well-bounded space—usually politically bounded —has left them unaware of some of the functional connections that a system-oriented metropolitan perspective might have provided. Emphasis on buildings or on specific place-locations has cut off consideration of the interactions that flow between places. And the protection of the future has shielded the planners from many of the short-run tests of the efficacy and suitability of proposals.

Into this climate the authors have attempted to pour the invigorating stimulant of the functionalism, tentativeness, and relativism of the social sciences. But social science alone will not win a better future for American communities. Nor will it revolutionize our image of future possibilities. It is apparent, however, that without its understandings, that image will be empty and misleading.

NOTES

[1] The city-planning uses of these methods and concepts are not unique. For a representative sample of recent ecologically based work, see Jack P. Gibbs, *Urban Research Methods* (Princeton, N.J.: D. Van Nostrand Company, 1961).

[2] For example, see the early critique by Milla A. Alihan, *Social Ecology* (New York: Columbia University Press).

[3] Herbert J. Gans, "Urbanism and Suburbanism As Ways of Life: A Reevaluation of Definitions," in *Human Behavior and Social Processes: An Interactionist Approach*, Arnold M. Rose, ed. (Boston: Houghton Mifflin Co., 1962), p. 639.

[4] Warren Weaver, "Science and Complexity," in *American Scientist*, XXXVI (1948), 4.

[5] M. Mead, "Values for Living," *The Metropolis in Ferment*, Annals (November, 1957), 10-14.

[6] See, for example, his "New Frontiers in Metropolitan Planning," *Journal of the American Institute of Planners* (August, 1961), 169-175.

[7] Robert B. Mitchell and Chester Rapkin, *Urban Traffic. A Function of Land Use* (New York: Columbia University Press, 1954).

[8] John Rannells, *The Core of the City* (New York: Columbia University Press, 1956).

[9] Martin Meyerson, "Building the Middle-Range Bridge for Comprehensive Planning," *Journal of the American Institute of Planners*, XXII (Spring, 1956), 58-64.

[10] B. F. Skinner, *Walden II* (New York: Macmillan, 1948).

[11] N. Long, "The Local Community As An Ecology of Games," *American Journal of Sociology*, LXIV (1958), 252 ff.

[12] Paper delivered at the Woods Hole Conference on Transportation Planning, 1961, under the sponsorship of the Highway Research Board.

[13] Raymond Bauer, "N + 1 Ways Not to Run a Railroad," *The American Psychologist*, XV (October, 1960), 652.

Index

Abercrombie, Patrick, 62
Accessibility, 85, 109
Ackerman, James S., 7
Activity, 227; hypothetical patterns, 141; interlocking subsystems, 55; specialization and location, 45-46
Adrian, Charles, 184, 196 n
Aesthetics, 33; adaptive approach to metropolitan planning, 69-70; afocality, 101; unitary approach to metropolitan planning, 67
Affinity, 106
Aided decision, 163; see also Decision, Decision chain, Market decision
Alderson, Wroe, 149 n
Alexandersson, Gunnar, 152 n, 219 n
Alihan, Milla A., 236 n
Aspatial, distinct from spatial, 37; related to process, 23
Artle, Roland, 7

Back, Kurt, 49, 75 n
Banfield, Edward, 77 n, 184, 196 n
Bauer, Raymond, 235, 237 n
Behavioral models, 54; Harris' view, 76 n; see also Models
Bertalanffy, Ludwig von, 147 n
Birchard, Ralph E., 148 n
Bit, 121
Blum, Henrik, 134
Blumenfeld, Hans, 148 n
Bogue, Donald, 139, 148 n

Brush, John E., 148 n
Building stock, rigidity of fixed investment, 39-41, 99-100
Bureau of Public Roads, 193
Burnham, James, 185, 196 n

Capital programming, 203
Center, 138
Centering, 84, 90; and activity specialization, 139
Central business district, 86, 104, 204, 211; decline, 214
Central city social problems, 211
Centrality of urban activities, 105, 202
Centralized governmental authority, 57
Central place theory, 83-84, 137-143
Channel capacity, measurement, 102-103; relationship to physical location, 98
Channel networks, spatial form, 97-99
Channels, face to face communication, 99
Chester County, 155
Chicago Area Transportation Study, 151 n
Christaller, Walter, 83, 116, 139, 140, 141, 142, 148 n
Churchman, C. West, 223
Citizen organizations, 179
City, as activity system, 227; as artifact, 225; as communication system, 86; place conception, 81-84, 108; as process, 200;

as social system in action, 93; as society of industries, 200; as society of people, 200; as static spatial arrangement, 89, 90, 92; as system, 75; traditional view, 81, 84; understanding lacking, 225

City planning, physical focus, 84; closed system, 223; see also General metropolitan plan; General plan, Master plan, Metropolitan planning, Unitary approach

Clustering, 106

Communications system, 97

Community, ambiguity of concept, 233; conceived as place, 108; geophysical base, 25; spatial and aspatial perceptions, 72; spatial, processual aspects, 6

Community organization, adaptive view, 65-66

Community Renewal Program, 228, 229

Conant, James Bryant, 167, 196 n

Concentration, 106

Construction statistics, 155

Consumer location behavior, 167

Copenhagen Metropolitan Plan, 63

Costs and benefits, 207

Cultural lag, 29, 39

Dahl, Robert A., 184, 185, 196 n

Dardick, Samuel, 151 n

Decentralization, 89

Decision, aided public, 163; analysis requires simplification, 222; building maintenance, 161; microlocational, 167; nonmarket oriented, 165, 188; see also Investment decisions; Market decisions

Decision chain, 171-175; conservatism, 175; custom as determinant, 175; interdependence of decisions, 175; steps involved, 172

Decision criteria, 164, 185

Decision package, 160

Decision process, professional standards, 193; role of high-level government, 188; technicians as communication links, 192

Decision system, mixed and open, 187; policy influences, 187; process aspects, 187

Decisions, interdependence of private and public, 228

Density, 103, 106; and interaction, 91-92; analysis, limited to site, 92

Detailed plans, 174

Deutsch, Karl W., 196 n

Dispersal, 214, 215

Diversity in associations, 112

Duggar, George, 7

Durkheim, Emile, 61, 77 n

Dyckman, John W., 5, 7, 149 n

Ecological models, biological base, 221

Economic efficiency, 49

Ernst, Martin, 234

European town planning, 63

Fabrega, Edwin, 151 n

Fagin, Henry, 7, 153 n

Festinger, Leon, 49, 75 n

FHA, 173, 193

Fisher, R. M., 150 n, 151 n

Florence, P. Sargant, 149 n, 150 n

Fingerhut, Jean, 150 n

Focality of interaction, 103-104, 131, 142, 143

Foley, Donald L., 7, 89, 95, 102, 148 n, 218 n, 230, 234, 235
Fried, Marc, 151 n
Friedmann, John R. P., 148 n
Functional interdependencies, 80, 97, 107; *see also* Linkages
Functional organization, aspatial aspect, 48-49; mediating device in community analysis, 27; no fixed relationship to values, 46; spatial conception, 44, 45; and values, 28
Future spatial pattern as goal, 57; *see also* General plan; General metropolitan plan; Goal plan; Master plan as product; Metropolitan planning, unitary approach

Gans, Herbert J., 151 n, 221, 232, 236 n
General metropolitan plan, 64
General plan, 57, 133; as policy statement, 22; *see also* General metropolitan plan; Master plan; Metropolitan planning, unitary approach
Gibbs, Jack P., 236 n
Gleicher, Peggy, 151 n
Goal plan, 199, 202; as objective, 208
Goal as process, 236
Government, disparity between ends and means, 215; high level, particularistic policies, 191
Government, metropolitan, *see* Metropolitan government
Governments, nonterritorial, 134-135; European Common Market, 135; United Nations, 135; United States government, 135
Government, territorial basis, 136

Governmental authority, centralized, 57
Governmental units, Philadelphia area, 162
Great depression, impact on planning, 65
Greater London Plan, 62
Gras, N. S. B., 148 n
Gravitation and potential theories, 45
Grodzins, Morton, 152 n
Guttenberg, Albert Z., 6, 7, 52, 76 n, 148 n, 218 n, 228, 230-231, 233-235

Handler, A. Benjamin, 49, 75 n
Harris, Britton, 53, 76 n, 148 n, 150 n, 153 n
Helfgott, Roy B., 76 n
Herbert, John D., 7, 153 n
Hill, Forest G., 77 n
Hoover, Robert C., 77 n
Housing market, 172
Howard, John T., 149 n
Hubit, 103, 121, 130, 150 n, 151 n
Hunter, Floyd, 182, 184, 185, 186, 196 n

Information flow analysis, 87, 97, 121; *see also* Social accounts
Information weighting, 130
Input-output analysis, 66
Insularity, 103-106
Intensity of interaction, 103, 106, 131
Interaction through communication channels, 96
Interdisciplinary collaboration, 43
Interest communities, 109-112; *see also* Urban realms
Investment decisions, criteria, 154; personal criteria, 166; political criteria, 165; macro-scale

and micro-scale, 166; public-agency approval, 175; technical determinants, 166; and urban change, 154; *see also* Decision chain; Market decisions

Investments, central city, 157; new, 160; public and private, 155; replacement, 160

Isard, Walter, 148 n

Janowitz, Morris, 184, 196 n
Jones, Barclay Gibbs, 147 n, 150 n
Jones, Victor, 151 n

Kaufman, Herbert, 96 n
Kent, T. J., Jr., 7

Lag, physical environmental, 39
Lapin, Howard S., 150 n
LeCorbusier, 63
Leibenstein, Harvey, 7, 150 n
Levittown, Bucks County, Pa., 176
Lewin, Kurt, 226
Land fundamentalism, 132
Land use analysis, activity component, 90-91, 101; behavioral-processual approach, 54; confusion of activities and physical facilities, 90; criticism, 90-92, 107
Linkages, 24, 55, 80, 83; analysis, 95-97 passim, 138, 149 n; *see also* Functional interdependencies
Local development controversies, resolution, 178-179
Localization, 106
Local government, 73; place base, 133-134, 226
Local leadership, conservatism, 177

Local planning, Philadelphia area, 176
Long, Norton, 231, 234, 237 n
Lynch, Kevin, 50, 51, 52, 68, 75 n, 150 n

Market data, 155, 170, 171, 194
Market-data services, metropolitan, 155, 189, 195
Markets as decision foci, 58
Market decisions, 187-188; components of rationality, 168; judgments entailed, 169; time, 169; value component, 169; weakness of fact component, 169; *see also* Decisions; Investment decisions
Mass communication, 86
Master plan as product, 224
Mead, Margaret, 226, 237 n
McKenzie, R. D., 139, 140, 148 n
Meier, Richard L., 7, 87, 121, 148 n, 150 n, 151 n
Metropolis as system, 21, 71, 220; *see also* System; Urban system
Metropolis, spatial and nonspatial aspects, 5
Metropolitan development policy, components, 191
Metropolitan government, 68, 73, 135
Metropolitan growth, 212
Metropolitan plan, 155, 190, 195; as functional analysis of realms, 145; for spatial interaction, 137
Metropolitan planning: adaptive approach, 57-63; analytic and empirical, 62; assumes future unknowable, 62; conception of plan and planning process, 61-63; concerned with organization and function, 60-61; deals with change, 69; evolution, 80;

focality and articulation, 68; the General Plan, 58; interaction and interdependence, 62; multiplicity of goals, 58; organizational view, 71-73; process emphasis, 58; spatial or aspatial approaches, 22; unitary and adaptive approaches contrasted, 56-63, 67-70; unitary approach, 56-57; weaknesses, 71; see also City plan; General metropolitan plan; General plan; Master plan

Metropolitan process, 80, 97

Metropolitan structure, 22; aspatial aspects, 24; conceptual schema, 24; evolution, 39-41; form and process aspects, 35; functional-organizational aspects, 24, 25; normative aspects, 24; physical aspects, 24, 25

Metropolitan transportation studies, 66

Meyerson, Martin, 77 n, 150 n, 218 n, 228, 229, 237 n

Middle-range bridge, 229

Minneapolis, 166

Minority groups, 190

Mitchell, Robert B., 7, 48, 75 n, 77 n, 148 n, 149 n, 153 n, 219 n, 227, 237 n

Models, marginal, 221; market ecology, 221; micro, 222; see also Behavioral models

Montgomery County, 157

Mortgage lending, 166, 169, 172

Mumford, Lewis, 77 n

National state, 220

Nation realm, 122, 152 n, see also Urban realms

Nelson, Howard, 151 n

New York Metropolitan Region Study, 52, 66

Nonnodal settlement patterns, 82-83

Nonwhite population growth, economic consequences, 190

Normative structure, 25; see also Goals

Nucleation of physical urban forms, 104

Ogburn, William F., 29

Open space, 42

Open system, difficulty of constructing models, 223; see also System; Urban system

Operations research, 66

Organization, characteristics of, 72

Organized complexity, 228

Parsons, Brinckerhoff, Hall, and MacDonald, 153 n

Parsons, Talcott, 76 n, 222

Pennsylvania General State Authority, 161

Penn – Jersey Transportation Study, 53, 77 n

Pennsylvania State Highway Department, 161

Perkins, G. Holmes, 63

Perloff, Harvey S., 5, 7, 77 n, 78 n, 149 n

Person, corporate, 56; private, 56; private vs. public, legal relationship, 197

Persuasion, 198

Philadelphia, 161; capital budget, 164; investment decisions, 161; local planning, 176; metropolitan area, 155; urban local governments, 162; urban power structure, 185

Philadelphia Chamber of Commerce, 171
Philadelphia Electric Company, 161
Philbrick, Allen K., 148 n
Physical, distinct from spatial, 43
Physical city, activity locus, 100-101; stability, 100
Physical environment, as artifact, 34; facilitates or impedes activity systems, 42, 45; permanence and stability, 27; provides mappable pattern, 27; relationship to activity, 32; spatially conceived, 44; symbolism, 47
Physical environmental determinism, 69
Physical facilities, fixity limits changing activities, 32
Physical form, buildings and adapted spaces, 99
Physical planning, see City planning; General metropolitan plan; General plan; Metropolitan planning, unitary approach
Place community, 79, 111, 113
Plan, end-state or process, 227; need for dynamism, 228
Planners, land preoccupation, 227; concern with means, 229-230; utopian tradition, 229
Planning, metropolitan; see Metropolitan planning
Planning, for open systems, 224; program planning, 43; social and economic, 43
Policy changes result from crisis, 181
Political city, 201
Political community, 201-202, 206
Population growth, suburban, 157

Power structure, 192; Boston, 185; diffuse and fluid, 182-183; information flows among groups, 183; New York, 185; Philadelphia, 185; Pittsburgh, 185; suburban, 186; variability of interest, 184
President's Commission on National Goals, 152 n
Process, 235; aspects of space, 37; aspects of urban form, 199; in decision system, 187; short and long term, 39
Public-information accounting; see Information flow analysis
Public investment, metropolitan areas, 157
Public policy, formulation over time, 180; public controversy particularistic, 181

Racial integration, 73
Radial highways, 204, 208, 210
Rae, James R., 150 n
Rannells, John, 48, 75 n, 149 n, 227, 237 n
Rapkin, Chester, 48, 75 n, 149 n, 227, 237 n
Rasmussen, Steen Eiler, 63, 77 n
Recreation policy, 180
Regional growth, 205-208
Regional Science Association, 67
Reichek, Jesse, 7, 77 n, 147 n
Relocation decisions, private, 207; see also Decisions, Investment decisions, Market decisions
Resources for the Future, Inc., 8
Reynolds, Robert E., 150 n
Robbins, Sidney M., 76 n
Rodwin, Lloyd, 50, 51, 75 n, 149 n
Role, 114; 150 n; self images of, 152 n
Russell, Bertrand, 79

Space, distribution of culture patterns in, 37
Standard Act of 1928, 64
San Francisco Bay Area Regional Plan, 139
Sayre, Wallace S., 184, 196 n
Scale, 47; relationship to norms, 34
Schachter, Stanley, 49, 75 n
Schussheim, Morton B., 7
Sedway, Paul, 151 n
Segregation, 106
Separation, 106
Shils, Edward A., 76 n
Siegelman, Lenore R., 7
Site qualities, 214
Sjoberg, Gideon, 75 n
Skinner, B. F., 237 n
Small-scale planning, 33
Social accounts, 87; and cultural progress, 88; *see also* Information flow analysis
Social ecology, focus on urban social systems, 220-221; overlaps space system, 221
Social policy issues, metropolitan, 73
Space, in sociology, 232
Spatial arrangements, and communication, 85; relationship to social organization, 29
Spatial and aspatial distinguished, 37
Spatial flows, 38
Spatial forms, 201, 205
Spatial pattern, 23, 24
Spatial-physical, 22
Spatial structure, dimensions, 103
Spatially structured process, 80
Specialization level, 113
Standards, 167, 193; redefinition and development by professionals, 194, 195
Stein, Clarence, 63

Stevens, Benjamin H., 153 n
Stewart, John Q., 150 n
Subcenter, 138, 206
Subcentrality, 105
Subfocality, 105
Subnucleation, 105
Suburb, 207, 211
Suburban power structure, 186; *see also* Power structure
Suburban shopping center decision criteria, 168; *see also* Decision, Investment decision, Market decision
Symbolism of physical environment, 47
System, 234; *see also* Metropolis as system; Urban system

Tactics, 198-199
Tactical city planning, 202
Tactical form, 210
Tactical plan, 199, 203; as action plan, 208; aimed toward city building, 211; attempts market control, 216; compared with conventional programming, 204; conflicts with conventional programming, 205; controls trends over time, 204; flexibility, 208; presents implications of goal plan, 217; resource allocation base, 205; strategy of control, 231; as urban renewal plan, 214
Tactical planner's focus on means, 216
Tactical programming, a technical matter, 217
Technical experts, 178
Technical standards, 174
Technological advances, 207
Terleckyi, Nestor E., 76 n
Toennies, Ferdinand, 61, 77 n

Trend estimation, 195
Trend interpretation, 189

Unitary approach to metropolitan planning, weaknesses, 71
Unitary conceptual framework of city, 89
University of Chicago planning program, 65
Urban economics, 67
Urban growth, complexity, 224
Urbanity, a function of information received, 88-89, 132
Urbanness, physical separation not criterion, 82
Urban node, 116
Urban patterns as field phenomena, 145
Urban-place conception, 81-82
Urban realms, 108, 112-132 226; analysis of activity system, 127; empirical observation, 120-132; form, 144; information weighting, 130; not spatially limited, 116; population composition unstable, 117; see also Interest communities
Urban realm map, 144
Urban region, 116
Urban renewal, 213; policy, 181
Urban structure, 43, 201

Urban system, 201, 222, 224, 225, see also System; Metropolis as system

Values, no fixed relationship to functional organization, 46; relationship to physical environment, 22
Vining, Rutledge, 148 n
Vitruvius, 147 n
Voss, Jerrold, 7

Walker, Robert C., 65
Warntz, William, 150 n
Washington, D. C., 190
Weaver, Robert C., 7
Weaver, Warren, 225, 237 n
Webber, Melvin M., 7, 54, 60, 76 n, 226, 227, 230, 234, 235
Wheaton, William L. C., 6, 7, 222, 228, 231, 232, 234, 235
Wingo, Lowdon, Jr., 53, 76 n, 78 n, 153 n
Wood, Robert C., 77 n, 151 n, 184, 196 n
World community, 113
World realm, 122; see also Urban realms
Wright, Frank Lloyd, 63
Wurster, Catherine Bauer, 7, 77 n